TRANSLATIONS AND TOMFOOLERIES

LONDON
PUBLISHED BY
Constable and Company Ltd.
10–12 ORANGE STREET W.C.2

•

INDIA & PAKISTAN
Orient Longmans Ltd.
BOMBAY   CALCUTTA   MADRAS

•

CANADA
Longmans, Green and Company
TORONTO

TRANSLATIONS AND TOMFOOLERIES. BY BERNARD SHAW

LONDON

CONSTABLE AND COMPANY

LIMITED

*First published 1926. Revised and reprinted for
this Standard Edition 1932
Reprinted 1947
Reprinted 1949*

PRINTED IN GREAT BRITAIN
BY R. & R. CLARK, LIMITED, EDINBURGH

CONTENTS

JITTA'S ATONEMENT

By SIEGFRIED TREBITSCH

Author of Genesung, Weltuntergang, Das Haus am Abhang, Tagwandler, Ein Muttersohn, Der Tod und die Liebe, Gefährliche Jahre, Spätes Licht, Die Frau ohne Dienstag, Der Geliebte, Die Last des Blutes, etc. etc.

TRANSLATED BY

BERNARD SHAW

TRANSLATOR'S NOTE

SIEGFRIED TREBITSCH, a well-known Austrian novelist and playwright, was born in Vienna on the 21st December 1869. The list of his original works includes eight novels and volumes of stories, and six or seven plays, including Frau Gitta's Sühne, of which the present work is a translation. I have to stress the word original, because, with a devotion extraordinary in the case of a writer with a successful career open to him as an original writer, he has undertaken and carried out the heavy additional task of translating and introducing to the German-speaking public and to the German theatre the entire body of my own works, both literary and theatrical.

This enterprise is the more remarkable because it was begun at a time when my position in the English theatre was one not of good repute, but of infamy. I was rated in the theatrical world of London as an absurd pamphleteer, who had been allowed to display his ignorance of the rudiments of stage technique, and his hopeless incapacity for representing human nature dramatically or otherwise, in a few performances at coterie theatres quite outside recognized theatrical commerce. Trebitsch knew better. He also knew English. He was quite unknown to me when he appeared one day at my house and asked to see me with a view to his becoming my interpreter and apostle in Central Europe. I attempted to dodge his visit by asking my wife to see him and to explain politely that a proposal to translate could be entertained only when made by the responsible manager of a theatre with a view to immediate production. The evasion failed ignominiously. My wife came to me and said that the young gentleman, though he seemed a very nice young gentleman, had swept aside her excuse with explosive contempt, and would take no denial. If I was to get rid of him (which she already regarded as doubtful policy) I must go down and do it myself. I came down; and the result was that the young gentleman carried the citadel by storm as successfully as he had carried the outworks. I did

3

what I could to dissuade him from what seemed a desperate undertaking; but his faith in my destiny was invincible. I surrendered at discretion; and the result was that I presently found myself a successful and respected playwright in the German language whilst the English critics were still explaining laboriously that my plays were not plays, and urging me, in the kindest spirit, to cease my vain efforts to enter a profession for which Nature had utterly unfitted me. In the last decade of the nineteenth century I was deriving a substantial income as a playwright from America and Central Europe. Not until the middle of the first decade of the twentieth could I have lived by my theatrical earnings in London. Today I have only to lift up my finger to attract a hundred translators. When Trebitsch volunteered for the job, the hundred would have fled from my invitation as one man.

It is not for me to say how far English drama is indebted to Herr Trebitsch for its present prestige abroad. It *is* for me to say that my personal debt to him is incalculable. When the horrible catastrophe of the war had torn Anglo-German relations to fragments, and only the fools who would not heed Mr Lloyd George's warning to "stop snarling" could doubt the vital European necessity for mending them, I could do no less than take advantage of the fact that Trebitsch has written plays of his own, to translate one of them from German into English for the man who has translated so many plays from English into German.

There were technical difficulties: how great I never realized until I took the job in hand. At first I was preoccupied with a quite minor matter. I can neither claim knowledge of the German language nor plead ignorance of it. I am like most literary persons: I have spent several holidays in Germany (mostly in Bayreuth), and have just managed to ask my way, and get what I wanted in the shops and railway stations, without the aid of an interpreter. The proverbial bits of Goethe and Wagner and Nietzsche are familiar to me; and when a German writes to me I can generally make out what he wants provided he uses the Latin and not the Gothic script. And that is all. When I opened the pages of Frau Gitta's Sühne, I was driven to the dictionary, only to discover that Trebitsch apparently does not use words that are in the dictionary. It was not by any process known to men of learning, but rather by some telepathic method of absorption, that I managed at last to divine, infer, guess, and co-invent the story of Gitta, or Jitta, as I have had to spell her to avert having her name pronounced with a hard G. Trebitsch is amiable enough to say that I have succeeded wonderfully; but even a very bad translation may be a wonderful feat for a translator who does not know the language.

However, when it comes to translating a play the mere translation is only the tiniest fraction of the business. I soon found that a literal translation would fail completely to convey the play to an Anglo-American audience. It was necessary to translate the audience as well as the play: that is, to translate Vienna into London and New York. And this involved translating one theatrical epoch into another. Vienna is still romantic in the manner of Verdi's operas, and modern in the manner of De Maupassant and Baudelaire. And as the conqueror always acquires some of the qualities of the conquered, even now that he no longer eats him, there is a touch of the east in Vienna, not only brought by the winds along the Danube, but left by the Turks when Sobieski drove them back from the gates. Add to this that Vienna has never weaned itself from the sweet milk of eighteenth-century art, when even woe was a luxury, and the heroine could not die in gloom too deep to please the audience. When natural history (sometimes ambiguously called realism) is banished from the theatre, cruelty, horror and death become painless there, and even luxurious, because nobody believes in them. The most frightful torments may be heaped on the heroine until she dies of poison or a broken heart: the villain may, like the wicked Count in Il Trovatore, live only to *centuplicar la morte* of the hero in *mille atroci spasimi*, and the hero himself may not know a moment of happiness or security until misfortune dogs him to his death; yet no one will turn a hair: the more dreadful it all is the better it is liked, because romance can never come home to

5

reality. To preserve this delicious anæsthesia there must be no bringing down to earth of the business by the disillusioning touch of comedy.

In England and America nowadays, such romance is privileged only in Italian Opera, and is not tolerated without the music. The Anglo-American audience wants a happy ending because it wants a credible ending, and therefore cannot bear an utterly unhappy one. It is true, as the late St John Hankin pointed out and illustrated by his Plays With Happy Endings, that the conventional happy ending is often as unhappy and disastrous as the marriages which foolish magistrates and police-court missionaries force on young people who have been no better than they ought to be. But the fact remains that in proportion as a play succeeds in producing an illusion of real life, it must dispense with the frantic agonies and despairs and poisonings and butcheries of the romantic theatre. Consequently, if you take a play written under the tyranny of a romantic audience and present it without modification to a comparatively matter-of-fact audience, it will miss its mark, and may even miss fire altogether.

To avert this result in the case of Frau Gitta's Sühne, I have taken advantage of the fortunate circumstance that in real life the consequences of conjugal infidelity are seldom either so serious as they are assumed to be in romantic tragedy or so trivial as in farcical comedy. I may as well confess at once that in the original play Jitta lives miserably ever after, and that her husband bears malice, and presents a character-study much subtler and more elusive than you will gather from my frankly comedic British version of him. Also Trebitsch, being a German poet, has a certain melancholic delicacy which escapes my comparatively barbarous and hilarious occidental touch. I could not help suggesting, by a few translator's treacheries here and there, that the ill-assorted pair settle down on reasonable human terms, and find life bearable after all.

Trebitsch goes so far as to say "You have made my last act almost a comedy"; but he is too amiable to reproach me, and tolerates my variations, which affect, not the story itself, but only the key in which it ends. Though the assumptions of the audience as to what will happen after the fall of the curtain will be more cheerful in England and America than they were in Vienna, the action of the play remains unaltered. Nevertheless those who can should read the original, to the idiosyncratic literary quality of which I have been shamefully unable to do justice.

Frau Gitta's Sühne was first performed at the great Burgtheater of Vienna on the 3rd February 1920.

Jitta's Atonement was performed for the first time at the Grand Theatre, Fulham, London, on the 3rd February 1925, with Violet Vanbrugh in the title part.

It was performed for the first time in America at the Shubert Theatre, New York City, on the 6th January 1923, when Jitta was played by Bertha Kalich.

JITTA'S ATONEMENT

ACT I

1920. *The drawing room in a flat in Vienna. It is fashionably decorated and elegantly furnished, but not homelike, as there are no books nor personal belongings nor household odds and ends lying about. The two photogravure reproductions of pictures on the walls, symmetrically placed at equal distances from the door, are of the refinedly aphrodisiac character considered de rigueur in hotels. But the place is not quite like a hotel sitting room; because there is very little furniture: only two seats, a couch, and a small table with a glass flower-vase and a mirror on it.*

It is an oblong room; and from the point of view of anyone looking towards the corner the long wall on the right has in the middle of it the door leading to the entrance hall; and the short wall on the left has an open door close to the corner through which a bed with rose-colored hangings is partly visible. In the same wall further forward from the same point of view is the fireplace.

The couch is in the corner, parallel to the longer wall, not quite close against it. A comfortable upholstered stool, really a chair without a back, is at the foot of the couch. This stool has a cushion on it which evidently belongs to the couch. The other seat, a chair with arms, is almost in the middle of the room, but nearer to the fireplace than to the door. The table stands near the corner of the fireplace.

It is almost dark.

Mrs Billiter, an elderly housekeeper, has something of the same undomesticated air as the room. Her hair, though not aggressively dyed, is still rather younger than her face. She is well dressed, like a hotel manageress. She opens the door, letting in some electric light from the hall. She has a silver tray in her hands, with a siphon, two tumblers, and a bottle on it. She switches on the light at the door, and crosses the room to the table, where she puts down the tray. She looks round the room to see whether it is tidy. She goes to the stool; takes the cushion from it; and puts it in its proper place on the couch.

9

Somebody rings at the outer door of the flat. Mrs Billiter goes out to open it.

A GIRL'S VOICE [*the accent is not that of a lady*] Gentleman ordered these. Suppose it's all right, isnt it?

MRS BILLITER'S VOICE. Yes. Just bring them in, and put them in the vase for me, will you?

Mrs Billiter returns, followed by a girl from the florist's shop, carrying a handsome present of flowers.

MRS BILLITER [*pointing to the vase*] There. I'll fetch some water.

She goes into the bedroom and switches on the light there. The roseate hangings of the bed appear to great advantage. The flower girl, on her way to the vase, stops fascinated.

Mrs Billiter returns with a jug from the bedroom washstand: a very pretty jug in rose color and gold.

The flower girl puts the roses into the vase; and Mrs Billiter fills it with water.

Mrs Billiter takes the jug back into the bedroom; and the girl steals after her to the door and peeps enviously in.

Mrs Billiter returns, putting out the bedroom light as she does so, and finds the girl at the door.

THE FLOWER GIRL. Just right for two, aint it?

MRS BILLITER [*incensed*] What do you mean, with your "Just right for two"?

THE FLOWER GIRL [*grinning*] Oh, it's nothing to me. But I know.

MRS BILLITER. You know too much, you do. Are they paid for?

THE FLOWER GIRL. Oh yes: thats quite all right. [*She grins again, shewing no sign of going*].

MRS BILLITER [*peremptorily*] Well? What are you waiting for? And what are you grinning at?

THE FLOWER GIRL. Aint the gentleman here? He promised to leave me something.

MRS BILLITER [*impatiently groping in her purse and extracting a tip*] Thats how they give themselves away, offering tips when they have no call to. [*She gives her some money*]. There! Now, out you go. I'm busy.

THE FLOWER GIRL [*sarcastic*] Sorry, I'm sure. Thanks awfully. [*She goes to the door, but stops on hearing the outer door opened by a latch-key from without*]. Oh, here is the gentleman.

The gentleman enters. The girl ogles him. He recognizes her, and makes a gesture towards his pocket.

MRS BILLITER [*very decisively*] Thats all right, sir: she's had what you promised. [*To the girl, sternly*] Good evening to you. [*She sails to the door so formidably that the girl, after an ineffectual grimace, has to go*].

The moment the gentleman is left alone he shews signs of severe physical suffering. His ascent of the stairs has brought on an attack of angina pectoris. He makes his way to the stool, and collapses on it, struggling with the paroxysm. Mrs Billiter returns.

MRS BILLITER [*running to him*] Oh dear, oh dear, has it come on again, sir?

THE GENTLEMAN [*a little better*] It's all right now, Mrs Billiter. I took the stairs too fast. I rush at them without thinking. [*He rises, and tries to take off his overcoat. She helps him*]. Thank you, Mrs Billiter. I—I—I— [*gasping*] Just a moment. Whew! [*As the coat comes off he plunges to the armchair, and sinks into it*].

MRS BILLITER. How often have I begged you never to walk upstairs but always to take the lift? And now see the state you are in!

THE GENTLEMAN. Dont look at me: it will only distress you. Angina pectoris is a horrible thing; but it passes off soon. You can do nothing, thank you.

MRS BILLITER [*taking his hat and coat out into the vestibule*] Dear! dear! dear!

Rather dazed by the attack, he sits up, straightening his collar and coat rather irresolutely, and looking very careworn indeed. He is well dressed, on the verge of fifty, going grey, very distinguished in appearance and kindly in manner.

MRS BILLITER [*returning*] Why will you never take the lift, sir? It isnt as if anyone in this house knew you. And for that matter you meet people on the stairs as well as in the lift.

11

THE GENTLEMAN. I know; but I mustnt let the liftmen see me coming here too often. People talk, even when they have to live by holding their tongues.

MRS BILLITER [*reproachfully*] Oh, sir!

THE GENTLEMAN [*quickly saving the situation*] Except you, Mrs Billiter. You are an exception to all the rules.

MRS BILLITER. It's you who are the exception, sir. I wish all the other gentlemen that keep rooms here on the quiet to enjoy themselves were like you. There are people and people in this world; and I know a gentleman when I see him. And I feel sure your lady is a real lady, and always the same lady; though of course I take care never to see her.

THE GENTLEMAN. Thats very kind of you, Mrs Billiter. [*He rises to go to the table*].

MRS BILLITER [*stopping him*] Now do sit quiet a moment, sir. What was it you wanted?

THE GENTLEMAN. A mouthful of soda water.

MRS BILLITER. There: I'll get it for you. Sit down. [*He does so. She goes to the table and fills a glass from the siphon*]. If you would only let me put a drop of brandy in it?

THE GENTLEMAN [*shaking his head decisively*] It would probably kill me. I know. I am a doctor. [*He takes the glass from her*]. Thank you. [*He drinks*].

MRS BILLITER. You are not right yet. I can see it in your face.

THE GENTLEMAN [*hands her back the glass a little abruptly, and pulls himself together*]!!!

MRS BILLITER. There! I shouldnt have said that. [*She replaces the glass on the table, snubbed*].

THE GENTLEMAN. Not at all: I know how anxious you are about me, and how kindly you mean it. But I am all right now; and I—I— [*he takes out his watch and looks at it*] I am expecting somebody.

MRS BILLITER [*taking the hint*] Yes, sir: I'm going. [*She crosses the room to the door, but turns for a moment appealingly before going out*]. But you will take the lift next time, sir, wont you? If anything were to happen to you—not that I think anything like that, of course; but—

THE GENTLEMAN. Of course not, Mrs Billiter. Still—[he *shrugs his shoulders*]!

MRS BILLITER. Yes, sir. And then what could I do but send for the police?

THE GENTLEMAN. Quite so, quite so. If I come again I will take the lift. I promise.

MRS BILLITER. Thank you, sir. Thank you kindly. [*She goes out, closing the door very softly behind her*].

The gentleman, left alone, rises and goes to the table, where he takes up the mirror and looks at his wrinkles and his blanching hair. He shakes his head and puts the mirror down. Then he takes out a cigaret; puts it between his lips; takes out a match, and is about to strike it when the bell rings twice. His face lights up; he throws the match and the cigaret into the fire; and goes out eagerly to admit the visitor, leaving the door of the room open. Immediately afterwards a veiled lady hurries in like a hunted creature. He follows her; shuts the door; and comes to her in the middle of the room. They embrace.

THE GENTLEMAN [*affectionately*] Why do you always look as if you were running away, and had just stumbled into my arms by chance?

THE LADY. I always feel as if my husband were lying in wait for me at the next turn.

THE GENTLEMAN. Well, suppose he were! You are not afraid of poor Alfred, are you? At home you are a perfect tyrant to him.

JITTA. I should have no courage if he caught me. Besides, if we are found out there will be an end of everything.

BRUNO. I almost wish we were found out.

JITTA. Why?

BRUNO. It would force us to stand by one another, and come out openly before all the world with our love.

JITTA [*embracing him impulsively*] Shall we?

BRUNO. There is my wife. Always my wife.

JITTA [*recoiling from him impatiently, and throwing her cloak on the couch*] Oh yes: Agnes. Always Agnes, Agnes, Agnes.

BRUNO. She has done nothing to deserve our betrayal of her:

13

she has sacrificed her life to me. I cant face what she would suffer.

JITTA. Has she sacrificed more for you than you for her? It is not the thought of Agnes that holds me back. But the scandal would ruin you. [*She takes off her hat, and puts it on the table*].

BRUNO [*with sudden energy*] I want to be ruined. Oh, the life of a University professor. His respectability kills his mind. His wife's respectability kills her soul. They both become mere shells of their former selves: going through life in grooves, on rails like tramcars, envying the tinkers and gipsies. If it were not for Agnes I should commit some disgraceful offence to free myself.

JITTA. I am afraid disgrace would not mend matters. I could not bear yours.

BRUNO. Nor I yours. We are in the net.

JITTA. Not here, Bruno. We have broken through the net into our dreamland. [*Now that her hat and veil are off Jitta is revealed as one of those attractively refined women whose wistfully sensitive unsmiling mouths and tragic eyes not only make imaginative men fancy unfathomable depths in their natures, and something undefinably sad and splendid in their destinies, but actually force this conception on the women themselves, however commonplace their characters and circumstances may be. Jitta is nothing more extraordinary than the wife of a college don, and has done nothing more heroic than fall in love with another and more poetic don (also married); but to her lover and herself her life is as dignified and beautiful as her face, and their relations as nobly tragic as her eyes. So, as we are all a little like that, let us share their dream for a moment whilst she continues, sitting down beside him*] You must brush off the bits of the broken net. [*Tracing on his brow*] There is a thread of it here, and here, and straight down here. [*She kisses his brow*]. No: they are not gone yet.

BRUNO. It is not the net. I can leave that behind when I come here into the dreamland. These last few months have been wonderful. But they have been terrible.

JITTA. Yes: wonderful and terrible. But they have been real, real. Life in the net is never real: it is all acting.

BRUNO. That is true. But there is something still more real than the dream.

JITTA. What is that?

BRUNO. The awakening.

JITTA. For me there will be no awakening.

BRUNO. There is always the tap at the door in the morning. The tap with bony knuckles. The caller.

JITTA. Death! Oh, why will you always harp on that? Death is nothing. Life with love is everything. Think, Bruno. We are here alone. There is nothing between us and happiness except the courage to grasp it. Can you never be happy?

BRUNO. Can any mortal be happy?

JITTA [suddenly prosaic and impatient] Yes: Alfred can. A glass of wine and a cigar can make Alfred happy. A vote of thanks can make Alfred happy. A cheque for £25 can make him happy. But I cannot make you happy.

BRUNO. Dearest love: you can, you do make me inexpressibly happy. So happy, that every time you go away from me, and I stand listening to your footsteps dying away in the distance—I always listen to them to catch the last sound of you—I am stabbed with a fear that I have held you in my arms for the last time. But when we have been parted for days, and I am here waiting for you and thinking the moments endless until you come, and at last I hear your ring, I suddenly become like a freshman just up from school. [She laughs, smoothing his grey hair]. Yes: I know; but grey as I am, I am still a hobbledehoy; just a student waiting for his girl at the corner of the street where her shop is.

JITTA [moved] And do you think it is any different with me? All day I long to be with you, to say a thousand things to you! And when at last— [she finishes the sentence by a caress]! When you are away from me, I plod through my housework, and just count the days until—until this [she again presses him in her arms, and draws him down beside her on the couch].

BRUNO. If only I were young! Then I could really begin a new life with you instead of merely thinking and dreaming about it.

JITTA. I like it better as it is. I dont want to see you every day and become a commonplace with you, Bruno.

BRUNO. But are you content with these heartbreaking stolen hours? I'd risk you becoming a commonplace: I want you to be a commonplace for me; but I daresay I should bore you.

JITTA [*sighing blissfully*] The happiness of these stolen hours is so delicious that it makes up to me for everything I have to endure between times. And who knows what would happen if I were to break up your home and shatter your career? Are you sure we should not be too tired out, too broken by the effort, to enjoy our rest? One has to be young to do such things, Bruno: young enough to be able to forget.

BRUNO [*sadly*] You are right. Our love looks well only by candlelight. It wont stand daylight.

JITTA [*refusing to be discouraged*] Daylight is for your work, for your great book that is to be the crown of your career. But here in the candlelight you belong to me, and to me only.

BRUNO [*quickly*] Oh, not here alone. Do you think that my wife and my daughter put you quite out of my head when I am at home? They never do: you are everywhere. But what must it be for you? I often reproach myself—

JITTA [*softly*] You mustnt do that. I am not unhappy, Bruno. I was at first: I hardly dared go home and face Alfred's inquisitive eyes. But he saw nothing: his self-conceit is impenetrable. His cheerful grin killed my conscience. I hold up my head now everywhere: I am proud of belonging to you. When one is really happy, one is ruthless and shameless.

BRUNO. Jitta: do you know that you belonged to me before we ever saw one another?

JITTA. Yes. We were destined—

BRUNO. I dont mean that. I mean that we actually belonged to one another physically. I mean that my daughter—born before we knew one another—is your daughter.

JITTA. Edith! What do you mean, Bruno? You have the strangest fancies.

BRUNO. This is not a fancy, Jitta. It is a hard scientific fact: I

16

worked out its theoretic possibility before Edith was born—before I ever set eyes on you. It strikes me dumb with wonder when I think how it has worked out between us. The daughter of my wife, my child and hers, not yours, resembles you, aye, loves you more than she loves her own mother, though she may not know it.

JITTA [*thoughtfully*] Strange. And I love your Edith as only a childless woman can love the child of the man she has interested and saved. I am not clever enough to share the rest of your science with you; but this I believe and accept. But how can such a miracle come about?

BRUNO [*mystically*] Men do not yet realize that no prophetic aspiration of theirs can fall utterly without fruit if its roots lie deep enough in their innermost conviction.

JITTA. Bruno: that must be right. It is an inspiration. It takes hold of my heart with both hands. You really are great.

BRUNO. Not at all: it is not new: everybody knows it nowadays in the rough. But it has never been worked out scientifically far enough to explain this miracle of Edith and you. Well, I am working it out; and there is somebody else working at it with me.

JITTA [*jealous*] Somebody else!

BRUNO. You would never guess who.

JITTA. I do not want to guess. I do not care.

BRUNO. Think of the most hardened materialist you know: the very last man you could imagine lending himself to such a mystical speculation!

JITTA [*relieved*] Oh, a man! The most hopeless materialist I know is my husband; and I do not want to be reminded of him just now.

BRUNO. But it is your husband I mean. I have converted him.

JITTA. Oh, impossible. He would never believe a thing like that. Dont let Alfred deceive you, Bruno. He is only playing with your belief because he feels sure of discovering some grossly material explanation of it, and making you ridiculous. He does not believe it as you believe it.

BRUNO [*brightly*] I do not say he does: I do not say he can. Alfred is clever; but he is not me—or rather, not us two: two in one.

JITTA. Darling!

BRUNO. All the same, he is burning with ambition to have his name connected with a new departure in science. As he has failed to do it in physics he is willing to do it in psychology rather than not do it at all.

JITTA [*scornfully*] At your expense?

BRUNO. Not altogether, dearest. He really has given me some quite handy curve diagrams for my lectures. He knows everything: what he lacks is a sense of the significance of what he knows. I am really sorry for him, and should like to help him.

JITTA. You can help him without letting him rob you of your ideas.

BRUNO. It is not he who is robbing me of my ideas: it is I who am robbing him of his wife; and the less he is conscious of his loss the meaner thief am I. I feel that through and through. [*He kisses her hand passionately*]. I have taken a priceless treasure from him. I must make amends somehow: I must pay my debt. That sense of obligation is in my very bones.

JITTA [*looking hard at him*] Why have I never felt this sense of obligation to your wife? Have I no conscience? or have you too much?

BRUNO. It is not the same. You do not feel that you have taken anything from Agnes: you feel that she has taken something from you.

JITTA. I know that I have a divine right to you. And I know that she has not.

BRUNO. There are other rights beside divine rights. If I had never come into your life, you would perhaps have come to some sort of understanding with Alfred; and he would have found some sort of happiness in possessing you.

JITTA. He has all the happiness he is capable of.

BRUNO. We have no right to say so. I have taken you from him.

JITTA. You have not taken me from him. I belonged to myself: and I gave you myself.

BRUNO. I have betrayed his trust.

JITTA. As I have betrayed your wife's trust.

BRUNO. That is quite different. Your relations with Agnes are mere society relations, conventional and superficial. But I am your husband's comrade: we were chums at school: we were at college together: we are professional colleagues. He knows me intimately; and if he were not such a confoundedly bad psychologist he would know that Nature meant you to be my wife. It is a stroke of luck for us that he knows nothing—if indeed it is only luck, and not his subconscious knowledge that he must not let himself know. Yes: he not only does not know: he will not know: he refuses to know. And that refusal, because it is unconscious, binds my sense of honor as if he spared us knowingly.

JITTA [changing her tone, and trying to soothe and coax him] Darling: you are tormenting yourself for nothing. Let me see whether I can cure you of all these scruples and fancies. They are only spooks. [She draws him towards the bedroom]. Come.

BRUNO. No, not yet. [He gets away from her by standing up. She shrinks a little, wounded]. I am telling you this once for all; so that I may never have to speak of it again. God knows it is not to involve you in my struggles with myself, nor to white-wash myself, that I am spending our priceless moments like this. I am as impatient as you are: I long for you beyond all expression. But there is something you must do for me. Something you can understand only when you know the rights of it.

JITTA [repelled and anxious] But what is it?

BRUNO [pulling himself together] I want to speak to you about my book. I have something very important to say to you about it.

JITTA [a little disappointed] Bruno: cant that wait a little? You know how I value your work; but we have so little time left this evening—

BRUNO [resolutely] It is just because I have so little time left that I dare not put this off any longer. You know the value of my book. Well, you must take charge of it.

JITTA. You need not trouble about that, Bruno: it will make your name famous without my help.

BRUNO [*looking hard at her, and forcing the emphasis of his words to the utmost*] Not my name. His name.

JITTA. God of Heaven! whose name?

BRUNO. Your husband's.

JITTA [*springing up*] Alfred's!

BRUNO. Listen to me. The book is finished: the typed copy will be found in my desk. And the title-page reads "Fetters of the Feminine Psyche, by Professor Alfred Lenkheim."

JITTA. Bruno! You are mad.

BRUNO. I burnt the original manuscript yesterday: there is not a word of it in my handwriting left to prove that I am the author. They will find a book by your husband among my things: that is all. [*She is about to protest*]. Promise me that you will leave this secret buried in my grave.

JITTA [*beside herself*] But why? Why? Why?

BRUNO [*seizing her hands, but now pleading like a lover*] It is my deepest wish. It is my most urgent prayer to you, Jitta.

JITTA [*gasping*] You ask me to do that! to promise you this unheard-of thing! This man who has no soul; who has been guilty of everything to me that a man can be guilty of to a woman except the infidelity that I would welcome with delight to excuse my own (he is not man enough for that): the fruit of your life's work is to drop into his mouth! And I am to be your accomplice in such a crime! No. I cannot. Never.

BRUNO [*soothing her*] I know how hard it is for you, darling. That is why I have not been able to bring myself to tell you until today. But I know you will not fail me.

JITTA. Dont say that, Bruno, as if it settled everything. I cannot act like a madwoman. Give me a reason.

BRUNO. I will. Listen. A book by a dead man is an orphan. Orphans sometimes die when they are not adopted. Mendel's masterpiece lay dead for thirty-five years while the fame of the

20

living Darwin spread over the world. If Alfred adopts my orphan it will not perish; for Alfred's wife will adopt it too.

JITTA. Oh, Bruno, Bruno, how can you? That is so clever, so damnably clever. Has it come to mere cleverness between us?

BRUNO. I asked for a promise. You asked for a reason.

JITTA. But I am thinking of your fame—

BRUNO [snapping his fingers] Psha! That for my fame! What does it matter from whose hands the new generation will take the torch to carry on the great race of science? The truth will be as true with Alfred's name tacked on to it as Bruno's.

JITTA [impatiently] Oh yes, yes: I know all that. It sounds like a sentence from your annual address to your students. It's not true, Bruno: I feel it. It is not human. There is something else at the back of your mind.

BRUNO. No—except this. When I finally and irrevocably sealed my resolution yesterday by burning the manuscript, there came to me a moment of extraordinary exaltation in which I saw this sacrifice as my atonement to Alfred. It is the price at which I buy his wife from him; and now at last I can take my happiness with both hands, free in my conscience, right in my heart, in all honor as well as in all affection to the very end. [He clasps her to his breast].

JITTA [still wondering at him] You throw the greatest achievement of your life to him like a bone to a dog; and then feel you have made us two one. [Breaking away from him] No, no, Bruno: you are asking too much. You know that I love you as my man, without a thought of your greatness and your work; but all the same your work, your greatness, are a part of you; and I love every bit of you, your body, your soul, your reputation, your work, everything that would not exist if you did not exist. All that is my treasure and my pride. When you take a handful of it and throw it into the mud, you make me so much the poorer. Have you thought of that?

BRUNO. When two people stand to one another as we stand, the children born from their intercourse are not always children of flesh and blood, but inspirations, intuitions, convictions that

21

they cannot discard without unfaithfulness. This is such an inspiration. Will you be unfaithful to it?

JITTA. Bruno: you want to play at Providence. Alfred is far too conceited to let anyone play Providence to him. If he refuses, what then?

BRUNO. He will not refuse. I have thought all that out. Why should he refuse to father a book which he already regards as half his own? He believes that I could never have written it without him. And you know how ambitious he is. I can depend on Alfred absolutely. Can I depend on you?

JITTA [half beaten] Who knows? I cannot depend on myself. This sacrifice is no child born of our intercourse, Bruno: you may be its father; but I am not its mother. I shall be its stepmother; and I shall hate it as no stepmother ever hated before. But the book is yours; and I have no rights over it: it must take the course you desire. I cannot go further than that. When you ask me to bind myself by a solemn vow, I— [shuddering] no, no: it is inhuman: a mockery, an impossibility.

BRUNO. I know I am putting your love to the cruellest test; but oh, Jitta, Jitta, do not fail me.

JITTA. So be it. [He snatches her hands and kisses them]. I promise you that if I survive the day that takes you from me, I will hide the truth as you demand, and take all the ghastly consequences just as you are mad enough to mean them. Are you satisfied now?

BRUNO [clasping her convulsively to him and hardly able to speak] I—I—thanks, thanks. My love.

JITTA [extricating herself quickly from his embrace] But if God wishes to be good to me he will never let me live to keep my promise.

BRUNO. I could not have pained you like this if I had the smallest doubt that I shall go first and go soon.

JITTA. Dont say that. Oh, do let us forget Death for one moment.

BRUNO. Death is nothing: if I could be sure that I should die tonight I should be unspeakably glad; for I should not have to strike you the bitterest blow of all.

JITTA. Bruno! Another blow!

BRUNO. Yes, another. My strength is going from me; and I need it all to force myself not to play the coward.

JITTA. How?

BRUNO. By leaving you today without daring to tell you that I do not intend to meet you again.

JITTA [*struck to the heart*] Not meet me again! Leave me!

BRUNO [*with deliberate emphasis*] This must be the last time. [*Rising, with a sudden fanciful recklessness*] Come: let it be the best. Let it be so full of happiness that we can say "It is enough: farewell."

JITTA. You are going to give me up! You can bring yourself to do that!

BRUNO. Nonsense! I shall never give you up. But it would be a crime to let you meet me here again at such a risk.

JITTA. How is the risk greater now than it has always been?

BRUNO. It was only a risk of being caught here with a live man. That was nothing: only a secret that three can keep. What about the risk of being found with a dead one?

JITTA [*about to shriek*]!

BRUNO [*covering her mouth with his hand*] Hush—sh! [*She looks affrightedly at him: he looks gravely and significantly at her*]. It is all up with me, dearest. I could not stop working; and my heart—

JITTA [*with agonizing anxiety*] Is it worse?

BRUNO [*with a ghost of a laugh*] Worse! It has gone all to pieces. I had no right to let you come this evening. I have put off telling you too long; but when I climbed those terrible stairs just now, I knew. You would have to give your name to the police. Our relations would be shouted through the streets and posted on the newspaper bills if you were found here with a—with a [*he cannot say it, and indicates, by a gesture, the figure of a dead man lying on the floor*].

JITTA [*flinching at the image, but steadfast in her thought*] Have no fear, Bruno. Why did you not tell me sooner what was troubling you? I could have relieved your mind. I have known all along that you were ill; and my only fear was that that [*she repeats his gesture*] might happen when you were alone instead of in my arms. Does that sound as if I cared what would become of me without you?

BRUNO. But I care, dearest. That is why I am resolved on our parting before this crazy tired old clock [*he taps his left breast*] runs down and stops ticking for good and all.

JITTA. Never. There is only one thing that can part me from you; and that is not the stopping of the clock, but of your love for me. No other danger exists for me; and no forethought of ours can protect us against that if it comes. [*Abandoning herself to her passion*] All the more reason why we must make the most of our love while it is within our reach. I love you: I love you: we are alive, not dead: you are living with my life as well as your own: your blood surges to mix with mine: you cannot die while I hold you fast. All the rest is an uneasy dream that means nothing: this is love; and love is life made irresistible.

BRUNO [*carried away*] Life: yes: this is life, and this [*he kisses her eyes*], and this [*he kisses her lips*]. What a fool I was with my iron resolutions! one throb of your breast, one touch of your lips; and where are they? Nothing matters but Jitta, Jitta, Jitta [*he kisses her again and again*]. I am neither weak nor afraid now; and I promise you to live a hundred years.

JITTA. All the unhappinesses are forgotten: they never existed. [*She turns him round and draws him towards the bedroom*] Come.

BRUNO [*beside himself*] You trust me; and I must betray you. You thought me a young man; and I let you think so. But you shall not be deceived. You have made me as young as I seemed to you. [*He seizes her round the hips, and lifts her up exultantly*].

JITTA [*terrified*] Oh God, no: take care, Bruno: take care.

BRUNO [*setting her down gaily*] Bah! Do I love you?

JITTA. Yes, yes. You love me. I love you. Come.

BRUNO [*pushing her towards the bedroom door*] Quick, quick.

JITTA [*running into the bedroom*] Yes, yes, yes.

BRUNO [*with a grim change of countenance*] Poor Jitta! That lift broke the mainspring. [*He staggers against the door frame; clutches at the wall to save himself; strikes the electric light out by chance; reels back into the middle of the room; and drops dead*].

JITTA [*running in: she has begun to undress*]What is the matter? Where are you? [*She stumbles against the body*]. Oh God! [*She switches on the light*] Bruno. [*She rushes to him and kneels by him*]. Bruno: speak to me if you can: is it your heart again? What can I do for you? Shall I try to lift you?

She tries to raise him by his shoulders; but they are too heavy. She puts her hand around his neck and pulls it up from the floor; but the back of his head remains hanging and his jaw drops. With a gasp of horror she replaces the head and closes the open mouth. Then she scrambles to her feet and runs to the other door, calling breathlessly and voicelessly Mrs Billiter, Mrs Billiter. *She opens the door, and regaining her voice, cries* Mrs— *She checks herself, suddenly remembering the consequences to herself of being found with the body. She closes the door quickly and noiselessly. She tries to think, her strained senses shewing in her eyes. Her fingers clutch for a moment at her half-naked breast as she thinks of her disordered appearance. She dashes into the bedroom, and reappears almost immediately with her blouse on, arranging it with nervous hands. She puts on her hat and mantle anyhow. As she turns to rush to the door the hat falls off. With a little cry of misery she takes the hat-pins from the hat and pins it properly to her hair; then she looks at herself in the mirror and shakes her mantle straight. She turns, and is hurrying to the door when she finds the body in her way. A flush of remorse comes over her. She turns impulsively to the vase; takes out a handful of roses; and is stooping to lay them on his breast when she realizes that a man who drops dead cannot scatter flowers on himself. She shakes her head and puts the roses back; puts her hands distractedly to her head in an anguish of perplexity, feeling that she must not leave him without some ceremony of love. There is only one thing that comes into her mind that will not compromise her. She goes to him, and cannot touch him or kiss him; but she makes the sign of the cross over him; kisses her hand; crosses herself; and hurries out, closing the door very softly behind her.*

ACT II

A week has elapsed. Bruno is buried, and his death from natural causes duly certified. Jitta has taken refuge in an illness, and is keeping her bed. Her husband, Professor Alfred Lenkheim, is sitting in his study after lunch with young Dr Fessler, who is engaged to Bruno's daughter Edith. Alfred lacks the distinction and heroic touch of Bruno; but prosaic as he certainly is, he is saved from being common, if not from being a little comic, by the stamp put upon him as a man of learning by his university training and his professorial Chair. His age is between forty and fifty. Fessler is just an ordinary nice-looking young doctor.

The room has two doors: one, in the middle of the wall behind the two men, opening on the corridor; the other, on their left, leading to an inner room. The window faces the inner door from the opposite side; and there is a window-seat before it. At right angles to this window-seat, further up the room, is a sofa. There are two tables: one a writing-table on the side near the window, at which the professor is sitting, and the other a round table on the side near the inner door. There is a chair at it with its back to the wall in which the entrance door is, and another, in which Dr Fessler is sitting, between it and the writing-table. The walls are crowded with book-shelves; and the writing-table is heaped with examination papers and manuscripts.

LENKHEIM. Whats the matter? Going asleep at your age! You were not called up last night, were you?

FESSLER. No. But, by Jimminy, Lenkheim, I have gone through a lot this last week.

LENKHEIM. How?

FESSLER. Just consider. Imagine having to console Bruno's widow when I'm engaged to his daughter!

LENKHEIM. Why not?

FESSLER. Because theyre at daggers drawn. Every word that soothes old Agnes is an outrage to Edith.

LENKHEIM. Why? Whats wrong between them?

FESSLER. Oh, Mrs Haldenstedt is old-fashioned. She keeps up

the convention that because Edith is a young unmarried woman she cant possibly understand about her father's death; and Edith has to pretend to be in the dark. But of course she knows as well as you or I; and it maddens her to have to hold her tongue and be treated like a child when all her feelings are boiling over about it. She was very fond of her father.

LENKHEIM. I knew the mother and daughter never got on very well together—jealousy, I suppose, as usual—but I thought this awful business would have brought them together.

FESSLER. Not a bit. It has set them more against one another than ever.

LENKHEIM. I suppose theyve no notion who the woman was?

FESSLER. None. She will never be found out unless she comes forward herself.

LENKHEIM. She wont do that. Why should she give herself away?

FESSLER. Women do, sometimes, God knows why! But meanwhile, poor Mrs Haldenstedt is most frightfully cut up. There she is, distracted by all sorts of surmises and suspicions, not knowing what to think, asking herself every minute whether he went on the loose and died in a vulgar street adventure, or whether there was somebody all along whom she never suspected, making her marriage a mockery. We are all as much in the dark as she is; for there never was a word against him: he seemed the correctest, most domesticated of men. That is, unless you know anything. You were so intimate with him, you know.

LENKHEIM. Was I really intimate with him? Certainly we were friends at college? and we kept it up afterwards. But he never told me much about himself.

FESSLER. He was not that sort of man. But he trusted nobody in the world as he trusted you: the widow is dead certain of that. By the way, she has asked me to prepare you for a visit she is going to pay you.

LENKHEIM. Why should you prepare me?

FESSLER. Well, she is going to ask you to act as his scientific and literary executor.

LENKHEIM [*pleasantly surprised and suddenly self-conscious*] Really! Of course I shall be delighted. I may tell you that in my own will I made him my literary executor. Who would have thought that he would peg out first?

FESSLER. But didnt you know that he was ill?

LENKHEIM. Oh, I knew about his heart and so forth. But many a patient with heart disease lives to bury his doctor. As a matter of fact his case was not a very serious one. His heart would not have stood racing up two or three flights of stairs. But does any man of his age race upstairs? A very strong emotion or excitement might have killed him; but a settled married man with a wife and a grown-up daughter suffers more from too little excitement than from too much. What emotions has a domesticated man of science to fear after forty?

FESSLER. Then why did he die?

LENKHEIM. Just so: why did he die? He wouldnt have died if he had been leading the quiet life we all gave him credit for. What sort of life did he really lead? That is the question.

FESSLER. Isnt it shocking that such a man should die under such—such—well, such shady circumstances?

LENKHEIM. Shady! I should call them disgraceful. Yes, my dear boy, we must face it: he came to a disgraceful end. An operatic tenor, or even a literary man, might be forgiven for dying in an adventure of that kind. But a man of science! Unfortunate, to say the least: most unfortunate.

FESSLER. At all events, since it was his luck to die in the dark, we are not called on to light the candle, are we?

LENKHEIM. We are not; but what about the police? And what about his wife?

FESSLER. They havnt the ghost of a clue.

LENKHEIM. It wont upset or delay your engagement, I hope. Not that I could blame you if you broke it off. Still—

FESSLER. *I* break it off! Good gracious, no!

LENKHEIM. I'm glad of that. Of course you must keep it up to Edith that there was nothing wrong.

FESSLER. But she wont have it that there was nothing wrong.

LENKHEIM. What!

FESSLER. You see, she adored her father. She sees him with a halo round his head; and nothing that he could do would be wrong for her. She has always felt that her mother could not live up to him; and she is persuading herself that this unknown woman was some wonderful person who made him as happy as she thinks he deserved to be.

LENKHEIM. Thats funny. Very funny. Does she suspect anybody?

FESSLER. I dont know. I cant see through her; and the worst of it is, she can see through me. She will find out what I think.

LENKHEIM. Which is?

FESSLER, Well, just what you think. And when she finds out what that is, heaven help me!

LENKHEIM. She wont find out. All that a young girl sees in a death is the romance of it: the vulgar reality does not exist for her. What an eye-opener for us who know better! [*Sententiously*] And yet, whatever view we may take of the affair, we must admit that these moral problems are very difficult: in fact, insoluble. Is there any man who can say that he has never been in a position in which sudden death would have been extremely embarrassing?

FESSLER. I suppose not. [*Naïvely*] By the way, that reminds me that I forgot to ask how Mrs Lenkheim is.

LENKHEIM. Oh, Jitta is getting over it. She hopes to be able to get up for a couple of hours today. Just in a dressing-gown, you know, to sit about a bit.

FESSLER. Oh, good. Well, I must be off to the hospital. [*He rises*]. Tell her I asked after her.

LENKHEIM [*rising*] I will. How soon do you think I may expect the Haldenstedts?

FESSLER. Any time now, I should think. The old girl wont be easy until she has seen you.

Lenkheim goes out for a moment through the inner door. Jitta comes in, languid, and dressed as Lenkheim has described.

JITTA. Oh, so glad youve come, Doctor. [*She shakes hands with Fessler*]. Have you seen the Haldenstedts? I was so sorry

29

not to be able to call on them. I have been really too ill. I hope they know that.

FESSLER [*with affectionate deference*] They thoroughly understand that. You must take the greatest care of yourself.

JITTA. You are not running away, are you?

FESSLER. I must. I have to be at the hospital; and I am late already.

JITTA. Come again soon, Doctor.

FESSLER. I hope to find you quite well then, dear lady.

He kisses her hand, and goes out. When he has gone, Lenkheim returns, full of excitement and curiosity.

LENKHEIM. Jitta: old Agnes is coming to see us. Bruno has made me his literary executor. That is what she is coming about.

JITTA. Has she recovered enough to bear discussing it with you?

LENKHEIM. She must. The world doesnt stand still when people die. I wonder what we shall find in his papers!

JITTA [*going white*] Has she found anything?

LENKHEIM. Yes: didnt I tell you? He has made me his scientific and literary executor.

JITTA. I mean about—about—

LENKHEIM. About his death? Absolutely nothing: Fessler has just told me so.

JITTA [*sitting down at the table, reassured*] Poor Fessler!

LENKHEIM [*resuming his seat at his writing-table*] Yes, poor chap: he is rather in a fright about Edith.

JITTA. Why?

LENKHEIM. He is afraid that her grief for her father will kill her feeling for him; so youd better take Edith in hand: you know how she clings to you. She is like her father in that: he clung to you.

JITTA. To me!

LENKHEIM. Yes: you know very well he did. If I had died you would have been up before this, I expect.

JITTA. Alfred: if you begin nagging I shall have to go back to bed.

LENKHEIM. Who's nagging? [*She rises. He jumps up apprehen-sively*]. There now: for God's sake dont make a scene about nothing. All I meant was that if he ever told anything to any-body he would have told it to you. [*She sits down again*]. Jitta: have you really no suspicion?

JITTA. Of what?

LENKHEIM. Who the woman was.

JITTA. How could he tell anyone who she was? It would have been dishonorable to betray her.

LENKHEIM. Men do tell, all the same. They dont tell the news-papers; but they tell other women.

JITTA. I object to be classed with "other women."

LENKHEIM. Oh well, it's no use talking to you if you will be so touchy. I didnt suggest that he told you: you brought that in yourself. All that was in my mind was that as you were so much in and out of his house you must have met her one time or another if she was the wife of any of his friends. It usually is a friend's wife.

JITTA [*with affected listlessness*] Is it?

LENKHEIM. Well, it stands to reason, doesnt it? Unless it's a chance woman from the streets.

JITTA [*wincing*] I suppose so.

LENKHEIM. Did he never talk to you about love, or anything of that sort?

JITTA. The last time we were at the theatre he discussed the play with me. It was a play about love.

LENKHEIM. Well, what else would a play be about? Thats no clue. I wonder was she a patient of his?

JITTA. Does it matter? Need we gossip about it?

LENKHEIM [*impatiently*] Dont be so superior. I like gossip. Everybody likes gossip. You like it yourself as well as anybody. If she was a patient that would account for his being so reserved about her.

JITTA. Alfred: you are unbearable. I will go back to bed.

She rises and makes for the door, but is checked by the entrance of Agnes Haldenstedt and her daughter, both in deep mourning. Agnes

31

carries a small dispatch case. She is not really much older than Jitta; but she has retired so completely from the competition of women in attractiveness, and accepted so fully her lot as a good bourgeoise with a home to keep and a family to manage on a slender income that she is set down as much older and less distinguished socially. Her sense of duty has kept her upright; and her uprightness has given her a certain authority, as of a person of some consequence. She has been deeply wounded by the circumstances of her husband's death, and is stiff and suspicious in her manner.

Her daughter is young and ingenuous, with a strong character. A passion of grief for her father has set her on fire with pride and a sense of being ready for any sacrifice.

The conversation which ensues is solemn, artificial, and constrained. They condole with one another in low tones and unnaturally bookish sentences. Jitta has to draw the girl to her, and kiss her on the brow. Alfred leads Mrs Haldenstedt to the sofa. When she sits down, he sits on the window-seat near her. Jitta leads Edith to the chair she has just vacated, and goes to the sofa, where she seats herself on the widow's left.

All these movements are ridiculous; yet the mourning worn by the two visitors makes them seem, if not natural, at least becoming.

LENKHEIM [*in hollow tones*] May I say again, dear Mrs Haldenstedt, how deeply I—

JITTA [*gushing*] At last, dearest Mrs Haldenstedt, I am able to tell you what I felt when I lay helpless, unable to pay the last respects to our dear lost friend. [*As she sits down, she seizes the hands of Mrs Haldenstedt, giving her no opportunity of refusing the attention*]. But in my sick room I was with you in spirit. Indeed I have never been closer to you and poor Edith than in that moment when I had to ask my husband to tell you what it cost me to stay away.

AGNES [*not at all disposed to allow Jitta so prominent a share in her grief, but conventionally resorting to her handkerchief*] Thank you. I'm sure it's very kind of you.

LENKHEIM [*clearing his throat and sniffing*] Under such a sudden blow, what can we say? We are all struck dumb. We all share

32

your grief.

AGNES. When people are sick, and we can sacrifice ourselves completely to the duty of nursing them: when they can lean on us to the very last, then, when the parting comes, there is some consolation in the thought that we have done all in our power. But an end like this, so sudden, so dreadful—[*she breaks down*].

LENKHEIM [*making the best of it*] Still, I am not sure that a lingering death really spares the feelings of the survivors. Death often tortures its victims before it strikes the final blow. In your case, dear Mrs Haldenstedt, there was at least no torture.

AGNES [*staring at him*] No torture! What has the future for me but the torture of a widow's grief?

EDITH [*unsympathetic*] It has the honor of father's name. Is that nothing?

LENKHEIM [*effusively*] Which I will help you both to uphold, my dear Edith, believe me.

AGNES. He knew he could depend on you. I have a packet of papers marked "Professor Lenkheim's property: to be given into his own hands": That is why I have come today instead of waiting for Mrs Lenkheim to call.

LENKHEIM. Dear fellow: how conscientious of him! such papers as he had of mine were of no consequence. Shall we have a little quiet talk all to ourselves, in here? [*He rises and crosses the room, inviting her, by a gesture, to come with him through the door opposite the window*].

AGNES [*pausing between Jitta and Edith*] I wanted to come alone; but Edith insisted on coming with me.

LENKHEIM. She was quite right. She is now your only support.

EDITH [*proudly*] Thank you, Professor. I wish you could persuade my mother that I could do much more for her if she would tell me all her troubles. I am no longer a child. There is nothing now that cannot be spoken of quite frankly before me.

AGNES [*with a weary smile*] Of course not, dear. But there are things it is better not to know. I know them; and I only wish I could change places with you.

Emphasizing this with an emphatic nod at Edith, she goes into the next room. Lenkheim follows her.

JITTA [*throwing off her false manner, whilst retaining the patronizing suavity of an older woman to a younger one, holds out her hands to Edith with genuine sympathy*] Come, darling. [*Edith comes to her and takes her hands*]. Sit here, close to me. [*She makes room for her on the sofa beside her. Edith sits down on her left, and looks gratefully and longingly into her eyes*]. Do you remember when we were last here together? Your father brought you. He was radiant with joy and pride in you. We were all so happy.

EDITH [*thoughtfully*] How long was that ago?

JITTA. Barely three weeks.

EDITH. It seems an age. I was a child then. I can hardly remember how I felt. It is as if I had been asleep.

JITTA. Your father's death has awakened you: you are looking at life for the first time.

EDITH. I have been looking at death for the first time.

JITTA. My poor child! But dont lose courage. Life lies before you: it will make up to you for many sorrows. You will get over it, Edith.

EDITH. Why should I get over it? I dont want to get over it. Do you suppose I feel disgraced?

JITTA. Oh no, no: of course not. But such a grief as this always makes us feel that we have come to the end of everything: that nothing can ever be the same again. Yet next day we find ourselves at the beginning of everything instead.

EDITH [*impatient*] You need not speak to me like that. You know very well that what is the matter is not merely the loss of a father: a thing that happens to everybody sooner or later.

JITTA [*taken aback*] Edith, dear—

EDITH [*downright and indignant*] Why do you treat me as if I were a little girl, as my mother does? I did not expect it from you. Oh, I am so tired of all this humbug. I turned to you because I hoped you would understand me, and let me open my heart to you like a friend.

JITTA. My dear: I will be an elder sister to you—

34

EDITH [*fiercely*] I said a friend.

JITTA [*surrendering*] Oh, you are terrible. I will be everything you want, if I can. But why are you angry with me? I really meant what I said. Life has a great deal to offer you: dont forget that you are going to be married. I believe you can trust your man. He adored your father. He will regard you as a sacred legacy.

EDITH. Thats curious. He used that word himself the day we buried poor papa. But I dont intend to be taken as a legacy, sacred or not.

JITTA. Edith: he feels your loss as deeply as you do yourself. Some of us perhaps feel it more deeply, because we have more experience of men, and know how much better what he was than you are yet old enough to know.

EDITH [*rising and pacing restlessly across the room*] Oh, these commonplaces! How you keep throwing them at me! None of us know what my father was: he was thrown away among us. [*Turning on Jitta*] Why did he not die with us? Why had he no last word for us? I was nothing to him: none of us were anything to him.

JITTA. You know, dear, that you are unjust to him when you say so.

EDITH. Unjust! unjust! what has that to do with it? Why did he not come to us for help, for nursing, for care?

JITTA. He was too considerate to let you know how ill he was.

EDITH. He told everyone else. We were left in the dark.

JITTA. No, no. No one knew it except himself.

EDITH [*passionately*] My mother wont speak to me about it; but I know very well what she is thinking. They whisper all day at home. I see it in the eyes of the visitors; and it makes me furious. I never want to see anyone cry again as my mother cried that night when they brought him home. It wasnt only grief: there was a bitterness in her that had nothing to do with grief or love. I have often felt in my soul that papa never found in his home what he needed and longed for. There were moments when I somehow got beyond myself and became another person; perhaps the woman I am growing into; and he was so responsive to

35

that flash of something different in me, so grateful for it, that I saw quite plainly how he was longing for something else, something more, than we were giving him. We were not good enough for him. [*She throws herself into the chair beside the round table, sobbing*].

JITTA [*rising and going to her*] Dearest: dont cry like that.

EDITH. It nearly killed me to see him sitting there, as he often did, staring right through me without seeing me, and sighing as he drew his hand across his eyes and through his hair.

JITTA. Dear child: you must not worry yourself because he sometimes looked straight at you and did not see you. Just think. He was a doctor: he knew his danger better than anyone. When a man finds himself condemned to death, his thoughts and feelings must be overwhelming. Well, if you were looking at the sea in a storm or at the heavens opening above it, would you see a tiny figure on the shore, even if it were your own child?

EDITH [*rising in a girlish rapture*] Thank you for that: it is beautiful, and quite true. [*She closes her eyes, silent for a moment, and a little breathless. Jitta smiles, and sits down in the writing-table chair*]. And now, wont you help me to find out the secret of his death?

JITTA. What secret?

EDITH. Who is the woman in whose arms my father died?

JITTA [*startled*] So that is what you think! Poor child!

EDITH [*angry*] I do not think it: I know it. You know it. Please let us have no more of the poor child business: it does not impose on me. How am I to find her?

JITTA [*remonstrating*] Edith, Edith, what could you say to her, even if you found her?

EDITH. Only that I love her.

JITTA. Love her! What for?

EDITH. For making my father happy. [*Restless again, pacing up and down*]. Oh, if you knew how infamously all those people who call on us misunderstand him. They insult my mother by condoling with her on her husband's unfaithfulness. They insult God by declaring that my father threw himself into the gutter, and was justly punished for it.

JITTA [*springing up*] What! They dare say such brutal things!

EDITH. Oh, not in those words: they are too polite to speak as horribly as they think; but I know. And my mother encourages them. She actually likes to feel that some unheard-of disgrace has fallen on her. She thinks it makes her interesting and revenges her. She positively wallows in it.

JITTA [*shocked*] Edith!

EDITH. Oh, it is the right word for it: why should I not use it? She never thinks of his sorrows: only of her own.

JITTA [*taking her arm persuasively*] My dear: you mustnt go on like this. Come: let me talk to you quietly. [*She draws her back to the sofa, and makes her sit down again*]. If you loved your mother as you loved your father, you would be kinder to her. You think of him as a man whose wife has failed him. Dont forget that she is a woman whose husband failed her.

EDITH. How did he fail her? If she had been worthy of him—

JITTA. Yes, yes, dear; but she was not worthy of him. Or stop: no: we have no right to say that.

EDITH. We have a right to say that she was not the right woman for him.

JITTA. Yes; but dont forget that that means that he was not the right man for her. He was her superior if you like; but that only made it worse for her. His superiority must often have wounded her self-respect; and as any weakness of his flattered it, she perhaps likes to think that he was not quite perfect, and even that he treated her badly.

EDITH. You think that an excuse for her! I call it abominable.

JITTA. Dont be impossible, dear. Abominable or not, it explains her readiness to believe the worst. You must not blame her because your faith in him is greater, and your consolation nobler. Remember: he did not betray you as he betrayed her. For he did betray her; and so did that woman. Tell yourself that, Edith, whenever you feel tempted to hate your mother. Promise me you will.

EDITH. I will never tell myself such a silly lie. I will take my father's memory and good name out of my mother's hands, and out of the hands of her tittle-tattling friends. I will make the world see him as he was, and as I loved him, not as she sees him, and as she hates him.

JITTA. The world will see him with its own eyes, dear, not with yours. All you can do is to save his memory from being blackened by that odious thing, a family quarrel. Come! promise me to stop worrying about your mother?

EDITH. I am not worrying about her: I am worrying about the woman my father loved. I cannot help it: she is always in my mind. Why was she not with him when they found him? Why did she run away like a criminal?

JITTA. Perhaps she is asking herself those questions every day in her shame and misery. Oh, Edith, we dont know what meannesses we are capable of until we are tried. The dread of a public scandal—of having to face a policeman prying into the most sacred and secret places in her soul—will drive a woman to anything. Remember: she had not only to save herself from the scandal, but his memory as well.

EDITH. No, no, no. She did not save him. She left him under the stigma of having died in the arms of some vile creature. I know in my soul that she was not that. The world would forgive him if it knew that she is what I know she must be if he loved her. Oh, why does she not defy all the silly world for his sake, and say "It was I."

JITTA. You ask too much from her. She may have been capable of great things when he was alive and at her side. What is the poor wretch now but a broken-hearted lonely coward?

EDITH. She is not broken-hearted: my father never broke any woman's heart. I loved him; and that makes even his death a glory to me. If she is lonely why does she not come to me? She shall come to me. We shall cure one another's loneliness, we two. Where is she to cry her heart out if not in my arms?

JITTA. No: she slunk away into the darkness. Let her be. She can bleed to death in her hiding-place.

EDITH. She shall not: she will be drawn to me: you will see.

Remember that I have no longer any place at home. I cannot live with people who cannot feel about my father as I do; and there is only one such person in the world.

JITTA. That woman?

EDITH. Yes. I will give her every right over me that the woman who returned my father's love should have over his daughter: the right I deny to my mother. I swear it.

JITTA. How serious you are, Edith! But what will your mother say, and the man you are engaged to?

EDITH. My mother would never understand: I take nothing from her that she is capable of missing. As to the man who says he loves me, and asks me to share my whole life with him, if he cannot understand me and support me in this he will never have me for a wife. I can do without any man if I can find the woman to whom I am bound for ever and ever. You will help me to find her, will you not?

JITTA [*deeply moved, drawing Edith to her*] Oh, darling, darling, if only I could! If only I dared!

Lenkheim throws the door open: he is returning with Agnes. Jitta and Edith move asunder and rise hastily. Agnes comes in, drying her eyes with her handkerchief. Lenkheim follows her solemnly with her dispatch case in his hand.

EDITH [*stamping*] Oh, bother! Always at the wrong moment. Always spoiling everything. [*She turns impatiently to the window, and stands with her back to them, fuming*].

AGNES [*to Alfred*] Thank God I found strength for this. It is a great relief to me. But I am dead tired: I must go home. [*To Edith*] Come, child.

JITTA. Wont you sit down and rest for a moment?

AGNES. Thank you; but I shall be better at home. And I have so many accounts to settle.

LENKHEIM. Ah, yes, yes: of course you have. Well, if you must go, you must. And you may depend on me not to keep you waiting too long before I go to work on the scientific papers.

JITTA. I hope to be allowed to go out again in a day or two. May I come to see you if the doctor says I may?

AGNES. Do, of course. I shall expect you. [*To Lenkheim*] You will forgive me, wont you, all the trouble I am giving you? It has done me so much good to unburden myself to a real friend.

LENKHEIM. You have had a cruel experience, dear Mrs Haldenstedt; but we must all resign ourselves to our trials.

AGNES. Yes: I suppose that is a great consolation.

EDITH. My consolation is that nobody dares console me.

ALFRED [*pompously*] Proud words; and how true! how true! [*Unctuously, as he shakes her hand*] Goodbye, dear lady, goodbye.

AGNES. Goodbye. [*To Edith, laughing a little maliciously*] Since you are so strong, child, just give me your arm.

JITTA [*shaking hands*] Goodbye.

Edith goes out with her mother leaning heavily on her. Jitta goes out with them.

LENKHEIM [*relieved at being rid of the widow*] Ouf! [*He carries the dispatch case to his writing-table, and sits down to examine its contents. He is in no hurry. It contains nothing but the manuscript of a biggish book. He leans lazily back with his legs stretched, and turns over the cover without looking at it. He reads a bit, and makes a wry face. He disagrees intensely and contemptuously with every passage he reads, abandoning each with sniffs and pishes, only to be still more disgusted with the next.*

Jitta returns; sees what he is doing; and halts between him and the round table, silently watching him.

Finally he gives the book up as hopeless; shuts up the pages; and stares at the mass of manuscript as if wondering what he is to do with such trash. Suddenly his expression changes. His eyes bulge in amazement.

ALFRED [*after a stifled exclamation*] Jitta! Jitta! [*He turns, half rising, and sees her*]. Oh, youre there.

JITTA. What is the matter? [*knowing only too well, and very angry at his contemptuous air, but pretending to be listless and languid*].

LENKHEIM [*shewing her the manuscript*] Look at this!

JITTA. Well?

LENKHEIM. Look at the title.

JITTA [*reading*] "Fetters of the Feminine Psyche." Is that the book you worked on with him?

LENKHEIM. I! Certainly not: he wrote it all himself: I only gave him his facts. Read the next line.

JITTA [*reading*] "By Alfred Lenkheim." I suppose he meant you to finish it.

LENKHEIM [*turning over to the end*] But it is finished. Look. Was he mad? Did he suppose I would condescend to put my name to another man's work? I have some reputation of my own to fall back on, thank God. There is something behind this.

JITTA. I suppose he wished to leave you something valuable as a keepsake. You were his friend.

LENKHEIM [*scornfully*] A keepsake! Dont talk nonsense, Jitta: a man does not give away his biggest work as if it were his diamond pin, unless he is afraid to put his own name to it. But if he thinks he is going to put mine to his trash he is greatly mistaken.

JITTA [*boiling with rage, pointing to the manuscript*] He has sacrificed his immortality for your benefit.

LENKHEIM [*angrily*] Rot. Why should he? Nobody who can create sacrifices his creation. [*He throws the manuscript on the table*]. Not that he ever pretended to think much of the book.

JITTA [*indignantly*] He thought the world of it. It was his greatest pride.

LENKHEIM [*turning on her, a suspicion flashing on him*] How do you know?

JITTA [*checking herself, feeling that her temper has betrayed her*] He often spoke to me about this book, and about the hopes he had built on it.

LENKHEIM. To you! What do you know about psychiatry? Why should he sacrifice his reputation to add to mine? quite unnecessarily.

JITTA. The whim of an invalid, I suppose.

LENKHEIM [*out of patience*] Whim! He throws away his one chance of notoriety; and you call that a whim. Do you take me for a fool?

JITTA. Dont shout, Alfred, please.

ALFRED [*subsiding a little*] I'm not shouting: I'm asking you to talk sense. You say he spoke to you about this. What did he tell you?

JITTA. Of course I knew too little of the work you and he were doing together to be able to help or understand much. [*Decisively*] But in any case you must carry out his wishes.

LENKHEIM. What wishes?

JITTA. You must accept what he has left you.

LENKHEIM. Why must I?

JITTA. It was his last wish: we have no choice.

LENKHEIM. We! Me, you mean. What have you to do with it?

JITTA. Well, you if you like.

LENKHEIM. It's not me youre thinking of. Funny, the way women run after a dead man if only he dies romantically! Anyhow this thing is impossible. I wont do it.

JITTA. Why?

LENKHEIM. Because it would be nothing short of swindling the scientific world to pass off his stuff on it as mine: thats why. And now, what the deuce am I to say to old Agnes? [*Grumbling*] Such an unreasonable thing to ask me to do! Such an ungrateful thing!

JITTA. Was it ungrateful to give you the whole credit when you were only his collaborator?

LENKHEIM. Collaborator! What are you talking about? He knew as well as I did that I was only waiting for the publication of his idiotic theory to tear it to pieces. You dont suppose I believe in it, do you?

JITTA. Then perhaps that was what he wanted to prevent.

LENKHEIM. Jitta: you are simply drivelling. Bruno was too jolly conceited to be afraid of me. Dont be childish.

JITTA [*irritably*] I am like yourself: I am only trying to guess why he did it.

LENKHEIM. Just so. Why did he do it? Where is the sense in it? I believe you know, Jitta.

JITTA. Really, Alfred—! I must go back to bed.

LENKHEIM. You havnt been up an hour.

JITTA. But I am dead tired.

LENKHEIM. You cant be as tired as all that. What do you want to run away for?

JITTA. Have you forgotten that I am ill? I can hardly stand. I must lie down.

ALFRED. Well, lie on the sofa.

JITTA. Dont be brutal, Alfred.

LENKHEIM. Bosh! You are hiding something from me: I havnt experimented with psycho-analysis for nothing. I notice that this crazy thing that bothers me doesnt bother you. You understand it: you couldnt take it so quietly if you didnt.

JITTA. I take it without shouting, if that is what you mean.

LENKHEIM. What did he say to you about the book and about his hopes? Why did you never say a word about them to me?

JITTA. I never thought about it.

LENKHEIM. If you had never thought about it you would have talked to me about it.

JITTA. I suppose I did not think it worth mentioning.

LENKHEIM. Psha! Would a man who told you all that not tell you plenty of other things? That love affair, now—?

JITTA [shrinking] Oh, Alfred!

LENKHEIM. Oh, stuff! Who was the woman? You know all about her: I can see it in your eyes. [He takes her by the shoulders and turns her face to face]. Aha! You know who she was. You know all about it.

JITTA [rising indignantly and letting herself go] You are mad, and grossly rude.

LENKHEIM [rising also] I have had enough of being humbugged. Who was she?

JITTA [closes her lips obstinately]!

LENKHEIM. Was he so much to you that you will not give the other woman away, even to me, your husband? Were those his orders?

JITTA [exhausted] I have no orders. I go my own way [she attempts to leave the room].

LENKHEIM [intercepting her] You shant run away. If you dont

43

tell me who she is, I will—I will— [*he makes a threatening gesture, not very convincingly*].

JITTA. Take care, Alfred. Your cunning is only a fool's cunning after all. The answer to your question is staring you in the face. Thank your stars you are too stupid to see it.

LENKHEIM. Am I? We shall see. Before you leave this room I will find out the part you have played in this dirty business.

JITTA [*starting as from the lash of a whip*] Dirty! Oh, never was anything purer, holier, nobler.

LENKHEIM [*screaming*] Ah! It was you! There was no other woman: it was you, you. He bought you from me, for that [*he bangs his fist on the manuscript*]. The damned thief! [*He collapses into his chair at the table, clasping his head in his hands*].

JITTA [*sitting down wearily on the sofa*] Leave the dead in peace. If you cannot hold your tongue, abuse me. I am alive, and can feel it.

LENKHEIM [*miserably*] You dont even deny it!

JITTA. No. Are you surprised? You lost me long ago.

LENKHEIM. My fault, of course. You worthless devil: what do you expect me to think of you?

JITTA. You can think what you like, Alfred. I dont grudge you that melancholy satisfaction.

LENKHEIM. Have you no conscience, no shame?

JITTA. Do you want me to make a scene for you, Alfred? I am sorry: I am too tired.

LENKHEIM. If I had him here—

JITTA. Threaten him to your heart's content. He is dead.

ALFRED. Yes; but I am very much alive. Dont forget that.

JITTA. Not so very much alive, Alfred.

ALFRED. Yah [*gnashes his teeth with rage*]!

JITTA. However, what I enjoyed I shall have to pay for. I know that.

LENKHEIM. You and he were lovers?

JITTA [*proudly*] Yes: you have found the right word at last. Lovers.

LENKHEIM [*whining pitiably*] And you could live in the house with me, and take my care and my nursing and my money, and even— [*He looks at her and chokes*]. How long has this affair been going on?

JITTA. Our love has lasted three years.

LENKHEIM. Love! Love in the sort of house he was found dead in!

JITTA. Love wherever we were. And wherever we were was paradise. Does that give you any idea of his greatness?

LENKHEIM. Of your meanness, more likely. Dont try to stuff me with big words: they only shew that you wont confess your caddishness even to yourself.

JITTA [*rising*] Oh, please! I cut a pretty contemptible figure—

LENKHEIM. [*triumphing*] You do. You do.

JITTA [*continuing*]—beside him.

LENKHEIM [*rising, goaded beyond endurance: threatening her*] You take care, do you hear?

JITTA [*wringing her hands*] My place was at his side. They should have had to tear me away from him by force. Yes; and I will tell you something more. The last beat of his heart would have broken mine if I had been any good. But I am no good; and here I am, as you see me. Oh, you are quite right. I have no right to be in any decent house [*she turns to the door*].

LENKHEIM. Stop: where are you going?

JITTA. I dont know. Into the streets, I suppose.

LENKHEIM. Oh, damn your heroics! You shant leave this room until you have told me everything.

JITTA [*bitterly*] Dont you know enough already?

LENKHEIM [*pointing to the manuscript*] What does that title-page mean?

JITTA. You know. You have said what it means.

LENKHEIM. I want to know what he said.

JITTA. That you are to be the father to his orphaned book. That the fame it will bring you will make amends to you—for me.

LENKHEIM. The blackguard! Not content with stealing you from me, he must dictate the rest of my life to me, as if I were a child.

JITTA. Yes: compared to him you are a child. He has provided for you.

LENKHEIM. Ha! And were you equally kind and thoughtful for his wife, eh?

JITTA [*earnestly*] Alfred: it was too strong for us.

LENKHEIM. What was too strong for you?

JITTA. Love. You dont understand love. Have you anything else to say to me?

LENKHEIM. No. [*He turns his back on her, and goes sulkily to the window*].

JITTA. Goodbye. [*She tries to go, but suddenly becomes weak, and reels against the head of the sofa*]. Alfred.

LENKHEIM. Whats the matter? [*He runs to her; and gets her safely seated*].

JITTA. Dont mind, Alfred. I shall be better soon: it is passing.

LENKHEIM [*turning brusquely from her like an angry child*] I am not sympathizing with you. It serves you right. [*He sits down at the round table, with his elbows on it, muttering and sulking*]. Treated me disgracefully. Disgracefully.

JITTA [*sighs wearily*]!!

LENKHEIM [*unaggressively*] Jitta?

Her name and the change in his tone give her a shock. She turns and looks searchingly at him.

LENKHEIM [*recovering his self-control by a rather broken effort*] This is no use. I have come to my senses. I—I will take it quietly and reasonably.

JITTA. I am glad you can: I wish I could.

LENKHEIM [*shaking his head*] But we cant leave it like this, can we?

JITTA. What can we do, Alfred?

LENKHEIM. You have done me harm enough. Do you want to ruin me as well?

JITTA. It is I who am ruined, as you call it, is it not? The sin is mine: I will pay the penalty by myself. Your life is only beginning: with that book you have a future. I have only a past. I will take it and myself out of your life. [*She rises*].

46

LENKHEIM [*out of patience, jumping up*] Look here: since you wont talk sense and be commonly civil to me, I'm going to assert myself. You cant settle an affair like this by looking like a martyr and walking out into the street. You must learn to consider other people a little. If you have no regard for me, at least remember that Agnes and Edith have a future, and have a right not to have it spoiled. For their sake I am prepared to endure your presence in my house.

JITTA [*with faint surprise and some irony*] You can bring yourself to that? You can still bear to look at me?

LENKHEIM. Make no mistake: all is over between you and me. For ever. I mean it.

JITTA. So do I.

LENKHEIM. Very well: be it so. But that does not mean that we need separate. People can live miles apart under the same roof. That is how you will have to live with me. If you have a spark of decent feeling left, you will not force a public scandal on me.

JITTA. Does it matter?

LENKHEIM. Does it matter! Are you utterly selfish? Dont you understand that if this miserable break-up of our marriage becomes known it will break up that poor woman's widowhood as well?

JITTA. Does she matter so much?

LENKHEIM [*playing his ace*] Well, what about Edith? Doesnt she matter? Do you suppose Fessler can afford to marry her if you drag her family through the mud?

JITTA [*staggered*] Oh! I was not thinking, Alfred. Give me until tomorrow to think it over. I can bear no more today. I can hardly stand.

LENKHEIM. You can stand as well as I can. [*She immediately sits down obstinately at the writing-table*]. Very well; but stand or sit, you dont leave this room until you give me your word to stay.

JITTA. With you?

LENKHEIM. Yes, with me. It is I who will have to pay the housekeeping bills. But dont be afraid: I am done with you, except before company. Not one word will I ever speak to you again when we are alone together.

JITTA. Oh, Alfred, you will tell me so ten times a day. Dont let us talk nonsense.

LENKHEIM. You will see. Not one word. Not a sound. I tell you I am done with you; and I wish I had never met you.

JITTA. It sounds too good to be true, Alfred.

LENKHEIM. Psha!

JITTA. But that part of it rests with yourself. [*Determinedly*] And now for my conditions.

LENKHEIM. Your conditions! Yours!!! You dare talk to me of conditions!

JITTA. You are in my hands, Alfred; and you know it. I can give the whole scandal away if you defy me. I will not be unkind; but if I am to keep up appearances, you must keep them up too. If I am to pretend to be a good woman, you must pretend to be a great man.

LENKHEIM. Pretend!

JITTA. Oh, be a great man by all means, Alfred, if you can. But you must pretend in any case.

LENKHEIM. How?

JITTA. You will pretend to be the author of that great book. That will be your share of the sham of our life together.

LENKHEIM. But I tell you I dont believe a word of the silly thing.

JITTA. Of course not. If you had the genius to believe it, you would have had the genius to write it.

LENKHEIM [*goaded*] I—

JITTA [*continuing calmly*] You cannot believe it, just as I cannot believe that you will never speak to me again;—

LENKHEIM. I never will.

JITTA [*still ignoring his protests*] —but you will come to believe every word of the silly thing, as you call it, when it makes Lenkheim as famous as Einstein.

LENKHEIM [*startled by the name*] Einstein! You are tempting me, you devil.

JITTA. You envied Einstein, Alfred. Well, all that you envied

48

him for is within your reach. Stretch out your hand, and take it.

LENKHEIM. And you envied Einstein's wife, did you? I see. Why could not your stupid husband give you a triumphant tour through Europe? Why should you not shake hands with all the kings, and dine with all the presidents, and have gala nights at the Opera? To get all that you will be my accomplice in a fraud, eh? Since you cannot have a good time with him you will have one with me.

JITTA [*round-eyed for a moment at this new light on her conduct*] How clever of you, Alfred! You have found a reason you can really believe in. I should never have thought of it; but you are welcome to it if only you will father his book.

LENKHEIM [*desperately perplexed: yielding*] But, Jitta: I dont really believe that. It's not like you: you are not clever enough, not ambitious enough. What is your real reason?

JITTA [*decisively*] He wished it: that is enough for me. He knew better than either of us what is best for us.

LENKHEIM. Did he indeed, confound him!

JITTA. He did indeed, Alfred; and I forbid you to confound him.

LENKHEIM. Well, if I do—and mind: I dont say I will—I—

JITTA. Yes?

LENKHEIM. I will think it over.

JITTA. Just so, Alfred. Goodnight. [*She goes out, tranquilly convinced that she will have her own way*].

LENKHEIM [*rushing to the door in a last effort to assert himself, and shouting after her*] If you think— [*He peters out; thrusts his hands desperately into his pockets like a cleaned-out gambler; trots back irresolutely to his writing-table; takes up the MS.; stares at it for a moment; and reads slowly*] "By Professor Alfred Lenkheim, Doctor of Philosophy in the University of Vienna." Well, I'm dashed!

ACT III

Mrs Haldenstedt is in her sitting-room with Alfred and Fessler, all three very busy going through the papers of her late husband. She is feverishly reading letters, and tearing them up and throwing them into the waste-paper basket as they prove one after another to be of no interest. Her sighs and exclamations of disappointment and impatience are getting on the nerves of Alfred, who is trying to read a manuscript. He flinches at the sharp sounds made by her violent tearing of the letters. Fessler, who is sorting some papers which he has already gone through, is sympathetic, and looks pityingly at the widow from time to time.

The room is lighted by a large bay window, with a window-seat under it. The table heaped with papers is in this bay; and Mrs Haldenstedt sits at the head of it with her back to the light, and Alfred and Fessler at the sides of it to her right and left respectively. The corner of the room behind them on their right is cut off by a double door leading to the study. Another door leading to the corridor of the flat is in the diagonally opposite corner, and is consequently before them on their left. On their right between the window and the study door, a console stands against the wall, with flowers on it, and above it a convex mirror. On the same side of the room, a couch.

LENKHEIM [*unable to bear the noise any longer*] Do you mind my taking these manuscripts into the study and examining them there? They require a certain degree of quiet concentration.

AGNES. I am so sorry. Bruno always said that it was like trying to work in a shooting gallery when I cleared up his papers and tore up useless letters. But if you dont tear them what is there to prevent the servants and everyone else from reading them?

ALFRED. Just so. But why not leave the work to us? Why worry? Cant you trust us?

AGNES. Oh, Professor, how can you ask me that? Of course I can trust you.

LENKHEIM [*nodding*] Good. Then do trust us. [*He goes into the study, and shuts the door behind him*].

AGNES [*alone with Fessler, letting herself droop*] I have gone through this last batch of letters three times over in the hope of finding some clue. But it's no use: theres nothing.

FESSLER. You mustnt worry.

AGNES [*sitting up sharply*] Have you ever lost anyone you really cared for?

FESSLER. Well, my poor dear father—

AGNES. I'm not talking about poor dear fathers or poor dear anybodies. Bruno was none of your poor dears: he was three quarters of my life, even if half of it was being his slave and his household drudge. All the same, I cant spend my whole life doing nothing but grieving, can I?

FESSLER. Just so. Of course not.

AGNES. Life goes on, doesnt it? Housekeeping goes on: the future has to be thought for as well as the past. All my business and responsibilities and duties go on just as if nothing had happened.

FESSLER. I'm so glad you have recovered enough to be able to look at it in that way.

AGNES. Doctor Fessler: a widow is not an invalid; and it doesnt help her to be treated as one when the first shock is over.

FESSLER. Quite so. Quite so.

AGNES. I am going to talk to you very seriously.

FESSLER. Of course. Of course.

AGNES. And you are going to talk to me seriously, I hope.

FESSLER [*surprised*] But certainly, my dear Mrs Haldenstedt.

AGNES. Yes; but that doesnt mean saying "Certainly" and "Of course" and "Quite so: quite so" to everything I say, as if you were soothing a baby.

FESSLER [*protesting*] But I assure you I—

AGNES [*gripping his hand on the table*] Tell me the honest truth. Did you consider Bruno a clever man?

FESSLER [*amazed*] Mrs Haldenstedt!!!

AGNES. Do you think he had anything to say more than any of the rest of the professors? [*Stopping him as he opens his mouth for a fresh protest*] Now if you dont, please dont begin to excuse yourself and spare my feelings. Ive had enough of having my feelings spared: I want the truth.

FESSLER [*whole-heartedly*] My dear Mrs Haldenstedt: he was a great man. His psychological doctrine was a revelation. It was the beginning of a new epoch in science.

AGNES. So I have always understood. I know he thought so himself.

FESSLER [*indignant*] Oh no: he was the most modest of men. I am sure he never said so.

AGNES. Do you think a man's wife knows nothing about his thoughts except what he tells?

FESSLER. I am quite sure he did not know half his own greatness.

AGNES. Then will you tell me what has become of it all? You and Professor Lenkheim have gone through his papers with me. Have we come across one word that could not have been written by an elementary schoolmaster?

FESSLER [*shaken a little*] Well, everything he wrote, even about trifles, has his peculiar touch.

AGNES. Everything he wrote is in his own handwriting, of course, if you mean that. But can you pick out from all that heap one single bit of paper which you could shew to a stranger and expect him to say "The man that wrote this must have been as great as Einstein"?

FESSLER. Well, not exactly Einstein, perhaps. But—[*he stops*].

AGNES. But what? Suppose he had left you a safe full of diamonds, and when you opened the safe it was empty!

FESSLER. Oh, you exaggerate!

AGNES [*rising, out of patience*] Doctor Fessler: if you can take neither me nor my husband's affairs seriously, I think you had better leave both alone.

FESSLER [*rising, greatly surprised*] Have I offended you?

AGNES [*disarmed by his naïve sincerity*] No, no. Never mind. Never mind. You are too young. You are not used to women. [*Sitting down again*] Sit down, wont you? I will talk to Professor Lenkheim about it. He will understand.

FESSLER [*standing stiffly, being now really offended*] By all means, Mrs Haldenstedt, though I really do not see what he can say more than I can.

AGNES. There! You are offended. But if you had been neglected as I have been for months past, while my husband spent hours and hours and hours in his study, writing, writing, writing, using up paper until it cost as much as the butter and eggs, you would want to know what had become of it all.

FESSLER [*sitting down again with a gesture of apology*] True. I should have thought of that.

AGNES. I never complained, because I thought it was a book that would make him famous and bring him in money. Well, is that heap of old letters and bills and prescriptions all that came of it? Dont tell me: there is a book somewhere; and I want to know where it is. Did he go mad and destroy it? If not, who took it from him? Did that woman?

FESSLER. Good gracious, Mrs Haldenstedt!

AGNES. Oh, this dreadful ending to all our happiness! It spoils everything that was nice in our lives. When the first and best of it was over and we settled down, troubles came I know; but I had my memories, and could sit and think of them. Now they are all poisoned for me.

FESSLER [*reflectively*] Dear Mrs Haldenstedt: may I speak quite frankly to you?

AGNES. Why, I am begging and praying you to. But I can get nothing out of you but sympathy, as if you were only a visitor instead of going to marry my daughter.

FESSLER. You see, though your husband will be remembered as a great psychologist, he had to practise as a doctor to make a living. Well, the wickedest and worst people have to call in doctors just as often as respectable people; and a doctor cant have them coming to his own house where his wife and daughter are. He has to keep a consulting room somewhere where they can come. The landlady said he rented the room to see his friends in occasionally. I daresay the women he saw there were common women; but how do you know that they were not his patients?

53

AGNES. Dont deceive yourself; and dont try to deceive me. Whatever I may have said when I was upset, I knew very well all along that Bruno never went with common women from the streets. The landlady said it was always the same woman, and that she was a lady. When she ran away she took that book with her: you mark my words. [*She rises and goes moodily to the console*].

They are interrupted by Lenkheim, who opens the door of the study and trots in flourishing a manuscript.

LENKHEIM. See here!

AGNES. The book!

LENKHEIM. I have just found an unfinished lecture on varieties of sleep.

AGNES [*disappointed*] Only a lecture! [*Taking the manuscript*] Why, it's only six pages. And what can it mean? There is only one sort of sleep.

LENKHEIM. Not at all. He says that hardly any two people sleep in the same way. Every case is an individual one. You must read it, Fessler.

FESSLER [*eagerly*] How interesting! May I look? [*Taking it from Mrs Haldenstedt*] Thank you. I'll read it in the study. [*To Alfred*] Mrs Haldenstedt wants to speak to you. [*He hurries into the study*].

AGNES [*shaking her head*] You see, Professor, it doesnt account for anything.

LENKHEIM. What doesnt?

AGNES. The lecture about sleep. He could have written it in one evening. Thats not the book that he said might be my best insurance policy. It was part of his provision for me. He would never have given it to another woman. If she has it, she stole it. [*She sits down on the couch*].

LENKHEIM. You are still worrying about that woman. I shouldnt if I were you. [*He takes his former chair, drawing it from the table to the couch*].

AGNES. I shall worry about her until I find out who she is. And I will find her out some day.

LENKHEIM. If it is any comfort to you, you may take my word

54

for it that with all his professional engagements it was utterly impossible for him to have given much of his time to any woman.

AGNES. What comfort is there in that? One hour is enough for a man. Then he can sit alone at his desk, thinking he is writing some great scientific work, when all the time he is thinking of her, living the hour over again, and looking forward to the next one, right in his wife's face.

LENKHEIM [*very uncomfortable*] Mrs Haldenstedt: do you suspect anybody?

AGNES. I cant see anything clearly. I thought I knew everybody that it could possibly be; but there's nobody. All I know is what he liked and what he wanted, and how easily he could get it by lifting up his little finger. Oh, I know exactly how he deceived us.

LENKHEIM [*rising, startled*] Us!

AGNES. Well, me and Edith, of course.

LENKHEIM [*sitting down, relieved*] Oh! Just so.

AGNES. She wasnt what you think she was, Professor: she was one of us. And I say that when a man has a wife and children and a home and a good position, he should think twice before asking any respectable woman to meet him in such a room in such a house. It was fit neither for him nor for her.

LENKHEIM [*drawing a little closer to her*] Dear lady: may I ask you a very indiscreet question? I shall not be in the least offended if you refuse to answer it.

AGNES. What is it?

LENKHEIM. Was your marriage a happy one?

AGNES. I always thought it was, at least until the last few years. Then there was a sudden change. Up to that time he was full of interest in his home, in Edith's education, in our plans, our money, the chance of our being able to move into a better house, the furniture and pictures, in everything. Then he seemed to get beyond us somehow.

LENKHEIM. What were the symptoms?

AGNES. Well, he was sometimes very irritable, though he used to be a perfect lamb. I thought it was only his health; for of course neither of us was growing younger. I know better now. Oh, what a fool I was! But that is how things happen. They go on from year to year under your very nose, staring you in the face; and you never notice, never think, because your mind is off the track. And then suddenly your eyes are opened with a bang; and you could kill yourself for having been so blind. If I could only find out who she was! [*She rises restlessly*].

LENKHEIM. Mrs Haldenstedt: take my advice: give it up. What is the use of tormenting yourself? You will have no peace until you put that woman out of your head.

AGNES. I dont want peace. I want to find her out.

LENKHEIM [*rising*] But suppose you do find her. What then? Think of the scandal. Believe me, it's better not to know. You could not hurt her without hurting yourself and Edith worse.

AGNES. I dont want to make a scandal; and I dont want to hurt her: I want to find out from her what sort of life Bruno was really leading, and what has become of all that work he did.

LENKHEIM. But the lecture on varieties of sleep—

AGNES. Stuff! I know the variety of sleep he learnt from her. [*Looking at him queerly*] Why do you want to prevent me from finding her out?

LENKHEIM [*meeting her eye with imposing firmness*] Solely for your own sake, Mrs Haldenstedt. How could it possibly affect me? Banish this abandoned female from your mind; and trust to Time. Time is the great healer. Time will restore your happiness.

AGNES. Well, Time works wonders, they say. But it will never comfort me until I know for certain that the happiness he had with me was the right sort of happiness, and the happiness he had with the other woman the wrong sort. How do I know that she wasnt a cleverer woman than I am? I dont care that [*snapping her fingers*] how young she is, or how pretty she is: Time will bring her to my level in those ways soon enough. But I'm not clever at the things he was clever at. I dont understand science nor care about it. If I have to keep the house spick and span I cant always keep myself spick and span; and I know he was particular about such things. Thats where she might have cut me out. She might easily have persuaded him that she was the right woman for him, and that I was the wrong one.

LENKHEIM. No, no. You were an excellent wife to him, Mrs Haldenstedt; and he knew it.

AGNES. I dont say I wasnt. But she hadnt to keep the house for him. She had nothing to do but please him. And if she was clever into the bargain, what chance had I?

Edith comes in from the corridor.

EDITH. Good morning, Professor.

LENKHEIM [*relieved by the interruption*] Good morning. Will you excuse me, Mrs Haldenstedt: I have a few words to say to Fessler before Jitta comes.

AGNES. You have been so good. I will think over your advice: indeed I will.

LENKHEIM [*encouragingly*] Do. [*He waves his hand to Edith, and goes into the study, leaving the mother and daughter alone together*].

AGNES [*looking after him bitterly as she goes back to her place at the table*] It's easy for him to talk.

EDITH [*wandering about restlessly between the table and the console*] Why do you listen to him? Why do you run to strangers when you want to talk about father? Why should our being mother and daughter keep us so far apart?

AGNES. What a thing to say, child.

EDITH [*going to her*] Of course if you dont want me, mother, I dont want to force myself on you.

AGNES [*dutifully, without real feeling*] Well, of course, darling, I want you.

EDITH [*irritated*] No, not of course, not in the way you think. Has it occurred to you that it is rather hard on me to be left entirely to myself when things are so serious with us?

AGNES. I dont know what you have to complain of. You used to trust me to know what was right for you, and now you have suddenly turned on me. Surely, child, nobody can be a better judge of what is best for you than your own mother. Here I am, worried to death almost; and you making it worse for me by setting yourself against me.

EDITH. I am not setting myself against you, mother. What I am setting myself against is being expected to go through life blindfold, or pretending to be blindfold. I am to be a good little child, and not know anything nor feel anything that little children ought not to know and feel, just when I, as a woman, most want the companionship of another woman to whom I can pour out my feelings and my sorrow on equal terms.

AGNES. I cant understand you, child; and I wont have you talking to me like that.

EDITH. I often wonder whether you have ever understood anybody. Perhaps you did not understand father.

AGNES. You dare—

EDITH [*continuing impetuously*] Oh, I know very well how tidy you kept his house for him, just as I keep my room. You did your duty: nobody can blame you. But was his house a home for him, as his heart made it a home for me?

AGNES. You are simply silly, child. Your grief and your crazy love for your father have turned your head. I wonder what you would say if you really knew.

EDITH [*scornfully*] If I really knew! Do you suppose any girl of my age nowadays does not know more than you were ever taught?

AGNES [*shrieking*] What?

EDITH. I know, as well as you do, where my father died, and how he died.

Mrs Haldenstedt covers her eyes in horror. Fessler, opening the study door, appears on the threshold.

AGNES. Oh, how dreadful! This will kill me. [*To Edith, rising*] Oh, now I know what you are. Just as bad as your father! Just as bad as your father!

FESSLER. What on earth is the matter?

AGNES. Dont ask me. Oh, this is beyond everything. Let me go [*she rushes from the room*].

FESSLER. What have you done?

EDITH [*coolly*] Told her I knew. I had to.

FESSLER [*closing the door, and coming softly to Edith*] My dear:

you have dragged the poor woman down from her little heaven.

EDITH. My father's wife might have had a heaven on earth; but that poor woman, as you call her, did not know even how to begin.

FESSLER. Your grief is carrying you too far. Try not to be unjust to her.

EDITH. I am not unjust. It is my father who needs justice.

FESSLER. It is not much use, is it, giving justice to the dead and withholding it from the living?

EDITH. You need not lecture me: I am on my guard.

FESSLER. Against what?

EDITH. Against sharing my father's fate.

FESSLER [terrified] Dying!

EDITH. No. Living in utter loneliness.

FESSLER. Oh, that! How you frightened me! But you know, dear, you mustnt worry too much about your father. It's a sort of hypochondria; and it may make you really ill.

EDITH [scornfully] Yes, I know. What cant be cured must be endured; so let us get away from this unfortunate affair and fall back into the current of everyday life. That is what you want me to do. But I cannot do it. He was everything to me: I cannot describe what I feel: it is as if I were a branch broken off from him, a limb torn out of him, as if I were bleeding to death of the wound that killed him. As I see him now he is quite different from what he seemed to me when he was alive, and much greater. I think of him imprisoned in these walls, longing for his proper happiness, and then finding too late the woman who was his real destiny.

FESSLER. Ah yes: destiny! destiny! He had to fulfil his destiny, I suppose.

EDITH. He did not fulfil it. Life fulfils destiny, not death.

FESSLER [prosaically] Well, you know, death is a sort of destiny as well. If you are right, and he really was lonely here owing to your mother being incompatible and all that, then I quite agree it was a mercy he hit on somebody who could understand him and comfort him. Still, you must be careful not to idealize a person you dont know. You see, everybody is an ideal person to us until we meet them; and then, undoubtedly, some of the gilt comes off the gingerbread. I am so desperately afraid that if you find her out, she will prove a horrible disappointment to you.

EDITH. Never fear. I know my father too well. [*Turning fiercely on him*] But that you can think so little of him as to believe what other people are whispering about him: yes, and about her: you! who have worked with him and had all his confidence! that digs a gulf between us.

FESSLER. Oh dont say that. You cant mean it, Edith. I love you. I have the truest respect for your father.

EDITH. Then how can you belittle him so?

FESSLER. My dear, I am a man; and I know more about men's ways than you do. A man is a very mixed sort of animal. Ask any experienced man, and he will tell you that there is a certain side to human nature that must just be ruled out in judging people's characters. Even the best men are subject to aberrations, or at least commonnesses, in their relations with women, just as they will eat rotten cheese, and half-putrid partridges that are really only fit for pigs.

EDITH. You are not making it any better by saying such disgusting things.

FESSLER. Yes: but you want the truth, dont you? You know very well that Goethe was a great man; but the fine ladies of Weimar were shocked by his marriage. Rousseau was a great man; but his Teresa married a groom after his death.

EDITH. My father was a gentleman. He was worlds above Rousseau in refinement, and even above Goethe.

FESSLER. Well, I could say something more; but I suppose I mustnt.

EDITH. What more can you say? Is it something more against my father?

FESSLER. Not exactly against him; but still—

EDITH. Well, still?

FESSLER. He married your mother.

EDITH [*staggered*] Oh! How mean of you to throw that in his face! Why do you not point out what is so clear to any unprejudiced mind, that a man who made a mistake like that once would be the last person in the world to make the same mistake again?

FESSLER [*with placid obstinacy*] Because I am sorry to say, my dear, that men's lives consist mostly of their making the same mistake over and over again. I see a lot of that as a doctor. Look at your mother: she knows that if she eats prawns and cucumbers she will have a wretched night; but she never can resist them. I knew a man who was married three times; and every one of his wives drank.

EDITH. The more you say, the more I see that we shall never understand one another, and that you will never feel about my father as I do. I could not have believed you could be so coarse. Nobody in this house understands me, neither my mother nor you nor anybody.

FESSLER. But if you want people to understand you, you must be reasonable. I often used to have to say that to your father. You take after him, you know.

EDITH. If I do I must take care not to make the mistake in marrying that he made. Doctor Fessler: I am sorry; but I cannot be your wife.

FESSLER. I dont mind that so much for the present if only you wont call me Doctor Fessler. It's ridiculous. You dont expect me to call you Miss Haldenstedt, do you?

EDITH. Yes I do.

FESSLER. Then I wont. You see, I dont know how long this mood of yours will last.

EDITH. Life is short: dont waste any more of yours on me. I shall not go back from what I have said.

FESSLER. Neither shall I. I can wait.

EDITH. I cannot prevent your waiting. Everybody seems to think they know my own mind better than I do myself. I can only tell you one thing. I have one object in life now, and one only.

FESSLER. And what is that, if I may ask?

EDITH. To find the woman who made my father happy, and to force you to confess that she is high heavens above your Goethe's Christiane, and your Rousseau's Teresa, and—you neednt remind me—above my own mother.

FESSLER. Well, I hope you may, darling. Does that please you?

Jitta comes in from the corridor. Fessler pulls himself together into his best professional bedside manner. Edith rushes to Jitta and embraces her.

EDITH. Oh, how good of you to come! How glad I am to see you!

JITTA. Is your mother at home?

EDITH. Yes: do you want her? I will send her [*she runs out*].

JITTA [*coming to Fessler in the middle of the room*] What is the matter with the child?

FESSLER. She is still fearfully upset. She is having a hard fight of it here.

JITTA [*looking at him with quick sympathy*] You are not looking very happy yourself, Doctor.

FESSLER. She has broken it off [*he narrowly misses a sob*].

JITTA. Oh, that mustnt be. Why, it was for your sake that I opened her eyes a little about her father.

FESSLER. I am afraid it had rather the opposite effect.

JITTA. I hope not. Tell me: does my husband know of this new turn?

FESSLER. Not yet. Perhaps you had better tell him. I dont know that I can go on working here every day if Edith sticks to it.

JITTA. Dont give in too soon, Doctor.

FESSLER. I am pretending not to—to her. But I am really afraid she may be in earnest.

JITTA. Is there nothing I can do?

FESSLER. It's very good of you, Mrs Lenkheim. But I must see this thing through myself, thank you. And now I must be off. [*He goes past her towards the door*].

JITTA [*shaking his hand*] Goodbye, Doctor. Dont despise my help.

FESSLER. Oh no, Mrs Lenkheim; but—

Mrs Haldenstedt comes in.

AGNES [*still distracted*] Oh, what is this that Edith tells me, Doctor?

FESSLER. We wont discuss it now, Mrs Haldenstedt. You had better talk it over with Mrs Lenkheim. Goodbye. Goodbye, Mrs Lenkheim. [*He bows to them and goes out*].

AGNES. Sit down, wont you? [*Jitta sits on the couch. Agnes sits down woefully beside her*]. He's gone; and Heaven knows whether he will ever come back. This is a marked house: everybody deserts it. Who knows how soon I shall be left alone here to haunt the place like my own shadow? I shall sit alone, going over and over that dreadful time in my imagination, with no relief but just thinking how I can catch that wretch that stole from me my right to be beside my husband when he died.

JITTA. She did not intend that. You may forgive her that, at least.

AGNES. Oh, you mustnt think it's mere spite and revenge. It's that I really loved Bruno to the last as I loved him from the first. He was all I had that I cared about. I am not like a man, to begin all over again with a new love: I shall never get away from it or get over it. Day by day all those years we lived together; sat at the same table; took it in turns to rock the cradle or take the child in our hands to pet it; and then he goes off to another woman without a word or a thought for me. [*Crying*] I didnt deserve it: I didnt indeed.

JITTA. There, dear, there! Dont torture yourself. After all, if he had died in your arms, you would still have had to grieve for him. It might even have broken your heart.

AGNES. Oh, if only it had! I could think of him then without bitterness and shame.

JITTA. Try to forgive him for the sake of the old days when you were young together. What does it matter what foolish things we old people do?

AGNES. I cant forgive him. Not while I am in the dark about her. Listen to me, Mrs Lenkheim. If I thought it was only her body that took him, I wouldnt care a straw. I have had thoughts myself about our young men at the college sports: only fancies of course; and I wouldnt have indulged them for the world; but a man might. What I cant bear is the thought that she might have been somebody like you.

JITTA [*startled*] Like me!

AGNES. Yes; for he thought a great deal of you; and if you had been that sort of woman, I might have been jealous of you. You are clever in his way; and you could understand him when he was talking right above my head. You could talk about his work to him. I couldnt.

JITTA. Oh no, Mrs Haldenstedt: I knew better than that. Nothing annoys a man more than a woman who talks to him about his business and pretends to understand it. Do you know what Bruno always talked to me about? what it always came round to, no matter what subject he started with?

AGNES. What?

JITTA. You.

AGNES. Me!

JITTA. Yes, you, you, you, you. Do you know, I sometimes wanted to shake him for not taking a little more interest in me occasionally? His conscience was never easy about you. You had done everything for him; and he had taken it all and gone on with his scientific work: the work that did not pay, when he might have been making a fashionable practice for himself and leaving you comfortably off.

AGNES [*beginning to cry*] But I never grudged it to him. I wanted him to be great. I wasnt really as good a wife as I might have been. I worried him about things that he neednt have known anything about. It's in my nature: I cant help it.

JITTA. It was not in his nature to blame you for that. He understood. He was frightfully faithful to you. You possessed all his thoughts: you dominated his destiny: you haunted him. What right had you to take a great man like that all to yourself? I wanted a little bit of Bruno; but you stood always in the way. Marriage is a very wonderful thing. It held him as nothing else

64

could hold him.

AGNES. But the other woman?

JITTA. Oh, the other woman! Need you make such a fuss about her? You dont even know whether she was not a patient who had to conceal the fact that she was consulting a doctor. There are such people, you know. But suppose she was what you think! Would a woman who had any serious relations with him have coolly walked off and left him to die? A pet dog would not have done such a thing. They would have found it at his side.

AGNES [*excitedly*] You think then that though he forgot what was due to himself, he didnt forget what was due to me? that when he went into that disgraceful place with another woman he was only making a convenience of her? that it was a mere chance that she was there to close his eyes, like a chambermaid in a hotel?

JITTA. She did not close his eyes. She stole away from his side after coldbloodedly covering up her tracks. Could you have done that?

AGNES. I never thought of that. Of course: of course. Yes: that shewed what she was, didnt it?

JITTA. What does it matter what she was? She came out of the dark, and went back into the dark. Leave her there, as she left him.

AGNES [*shaking her head*] I cant imagine how women can bring themselves to behave so. What sort of women must they be? She must have known that he could never have cared for her.

JITTA. You dont know how she got him there. But I know that if he really opened his heart to her, he talked to her about you.

AGNES [*smiling*] Well, I am sure, Mrs Lenkheim, this talk has made the most wonderful difference to me. You dont know how much good you have done me. It only shews how little we can trust our own feelings and our own judgment when such troubles come to us. The weight you have taken off my mind! you cant imagine.

JITTA. Have I? Then I have done what I came to do. [*She rises*].

AGNES [*holding her*] Oh, dont go yet. You know, it's very funny how one's mind works.

65   F

JITTA [*sitting down again*] How?

AGNES [*slowly and almost roguishly*] I'm so grateful to you, that I'm afraid of offending you if I tell you. But I am sure you will only laugh.

JITTA [*with a melancholy smile*] We both need a good laugh, dont we?

AGNES. Have you ever found that you have been all along thinking something that never came into your head for a single moment?

JITTA. That sounds a little difficult. I am afraid I dont quite follow.

AGNES. Of course you dont: it's too silly. But do you know that the moment you took that weight off my mind, and gave me back my peace and happiness—

JITTA [*murmurs*] I am so glad that I did.

AGNES [*nodding gratefully, and continuing*] Well, that very moment I knew that I had been believing all along—but I dont think I ought to say it; only it's so funny.

JITTA. What?

AGNES. Why, that YOU were the woman. [*She begins to chuckle*].

JITTA. No!!!

AGNES. Yes I did.

JITTA. But really?

AGNES. Really and truly.

JITTA [*beginning to laugh hysterically*] How funny!

AGNES [*her chuckles now culminating in hearty laughter*] Isnt it? Youre not angry, are you? Oh dear—[*laughing more than ever*].

JITTA. Oh no: of course not.

Jitta has a paroxysm of agonizing laughter; and Agnes accompanies her without a suspicion that she is not enjoying the joke in good faith. Jitta at last recovers her self-control with a desperate effort.

JITTA. Dont make me laugh any more: I am afraid I shall go into hysterics. I am still very far from well.

AGNES. It's such a shame to laugh at all at such a time. But for the life of me I couldnt help it.

JITTA [*looking hard at her*] You know, Mrs Haldenstedt, I was very very fond of him.

AGNES. I am sure you were, darling; and I shouldnt have minded a bit if it had been you: in fact I'm half disappointed that it wasnt, you have been such an angel to me. Isnt it funny, the things that come into our heads? But it's wicked of me to make you talk and laugh so much, and you so ill. Youre very pale, dear. Can I get you anything?

JITTA. If I might just lie down here for awhile. I—

AGNES [*rising to make room for Jitta to recline*] Yes, yes: of course you shall, dear. Make yourself comfortable.

JITTA. I dont want to go without seeing Edith.

AGNES [*taken aback*] Oh!

JITTA. What is it?

AGNES. I forgot all about Edith. Who is to tell her? She sees her father like a saint in a picture; and I could never put it to her in the wonderful way you put it to me. If only you would be so good as to tell her for me. Would you mind?

JITTA. Not in the least. Edith is like a child of my own to me: it would be the greatest happiness to me if I could set her mind at rest as you are good enough to think I have set yours.

AGNES. You have: indeed and indeed you have. I am sure what we owe you, with your dear husband coming here every day to set the papers in order, and you being more than an angel to me in spite of your illness, words can never say. Just lie quiet where you are; and I will send Edith to you. Oh, you have made me happy, dear! [*She goes out into the corridor*].

Jitta, left alone, begins to laugh again hysterically, and is dissolving into convulsive sobs when she makes a great effort; springs up from the sofa; dashes the tears from her eyes with a proud gesture; goes to the glass; and has just made herself presentable when Edith appears. Her eyes are wide open and her expression one of joyful surprise and relief. She runs eagerly to Jitta.

EDITH. What on earth have you done to mother? She is laughing. She is positively singing. Either you are a witch, or she has gone mad.

JITTA. Are you angry with her for daring to sing in this house of mourning? Or angry with me for making her sing?

EDITH. Oh no: it's rather a relief. But it's very odd. How did you do it?

JITTA. She made me laugh before I made her sing. You mustnt be shocked, dear. There is always a sort of reaction: Nature must have a relief from any feeling, no matter how deep and sincere it is. Have you ever seen a soldier's funeral?

EDITH. No. Why?

JITTA. They play the Dead March as they go to the grave; but they play the merriest tunes they know on their way back.

EDITH. How unfeeling!

JITTA. Yes; but how natural! Your mother would have gone mad if she had gone on as she was for another week. I am not sure that I should not have gone mad myself if she had not made me laugh. [*Taking Edith by the shoulders and looking straight at her*] And now what I want to know is how I am to make you laugh. For you will go mad if you do not get back into everyday life again.

EDITH [*backing to the table, and half sitting against its edge*] Yes: I know. This house has been a sort of madhouse since my father died. We havnt spoken naturally, nor walked naturally, nor breathed naturally, nor thought naturally, because we were all so determined to feel naturally. Somehow, my mother's laughing and singing has made nonsense of it all suddenly.

JITTA. Then you are happy again? If so, I may as well go home.

EDITH. Happy! Oh no. But I am done with hypocrisy and conventionality; and that is such a relief that I seem happy by contrast. I suppose it is a sort of happiness to be able to give myself up at last wholly to my sorrow.

JITTA [*sitting down in Lenkheim's chair*] Which sorrow? The old sorrow that God made for you, or the new one that you have made for yourself?

EDITH [*straightening up*] I dont know what you mean.

JITTA. Doctor Fessler says you have jilted him.

68

EDITH. Did he call it jilting him?

JITTA. No. I call it that.

EDITH. But you cant think that. Do you know what he said?

JITTA. No. Anything very dreadful?

EDITH. He believes that my father died in the arms of a common woman of the streets.

JITTA. And he thinks your father must have been as worthless as the woman he died with. I see.

EDITH. Not at all. That is what is so dreadful. He thinks it makes no difference. He adores my father as much as he ever did; but he thinks you have to leave all that out when you are judging men. He thinks a woman doesnt matter. I cant forgive him for that. I couldnt marry a man unless he felt exactly as I do about my father.

JITTA. Is that reasonable, dear? How could poor Doctor Fessler feel as you feel? you! your father's daughter!

EDITH. Oh, of course I know that. I dont expect him to feel the same affection. But if he thought my father could go with low women—if he did not know for certain, as I know, that the woman my father loved must have been one of the best and noblest of women, I would rather die than let him touch me.

JITTA. My dear: how can he know for certain? You do not know for certain yourself.

EDITH. I know I cant prove it. But I am certain. And I will devote my life to proving it.

JITTA. How?

EDITH. I will find the woman: that is how. I have thought and thought about it. I know that she cannot be very far off. I know that her grief and desolation must be as great as mine: greater. I know she will love me because I am his daughter. And I know that she will be somebody worthy of him.

JITTA. Edith, Edith, how sentimental you are!

EDITH [fiercely] You call my feeling sentimentality! Are you going to disappoint me too?

JITTA [sternly] You must learn to expect disappointments. How do you know that if you found this woman she would not disappoint you? It is easy to imagine wonderful women worthy of your father's love. But the real person always kills the imagined person.

EDITH. He said that once.

JITTA. Well, is it not true? Can you think of any real woman among your acquaintances that you could bear to think of as that woman—even the best of them?

EDITH. You cant put me off that way. I tell you I know. There is some woman who was real to my father; and he loved her. I shall love her when she is real to me. Besides, I have a queer sense that I know her quite as well as a real person; that she is here within reach of my hands if only I could recollect. I—I sometimes wonder does everybody know? does my mother know?

JITTA [quickly] Your mother does not know. Your mother could never understand.

EDITH. Jitta: do you know?

JITTA. Yes.

EDITH. Jitta!!!

JITTA. Yes. I know that poor criminal. I know what has become of her. I know what she did. I know what she has suffered ever since.

EDITH. But how do you know? Oh, tell me. You must tell me now.

JITTA. When you are excited like that your voice is his voice. Oh, the agony of hearing it, and the happiness! You bring him to life again for me.

EDITH. Then it was—

JITTA. Only me, dear.

EDITH [flinging herself into Jitta's arms] Only you! Who better could it be? Of course it was you. I knew it all along, only I couldnt recollect. Oh, darling! Dont you want a daughter? Here I am. His daughter.

JITTA. Dearest, yes. You have been a daughter to me ever since I knew him. But we must be very careful, very discreet. You see, you are very young.

EDITH. Oh, dont begin that. I dont want that sort of mother.

JITTA. I know. But I mustnt take your devotion—it is devotion, isnt it?—

EDITH. Oh yes, yes.

JITTA. I mustnt take it under false pretences. Above all, you must not throw away your engagement because your lover does not feel about me as you do. He is right about me, you know: I am not a good woman. Have you quite forgotten that *I* have a husband, and that for your father's sake I was unfaithful to him?

EDITH [*naïvely*] Oh, but Alfred is such a chump!

JITTA [*a little shocked*] Edith!

EDITH. And papa was such a wonderful man! Nobody could blame you.

JITTA. I assure you a great many people would blame me so much that they would never speak to me again if they knew.

EDITH. More shame for them! Do such people matter?

JITTA. They do, dear. I am afraid they are the only people who do matter in this wretched world. So you musnt tell them. You mustnt tell anybody.

EDITH [*slowly*] I suppose not.

JITTA. Did you intend to tell everybody?

EDITH. No, of course not: I am not such a fool as that. But I did think that if I told Doctor Fessler he might see that he was wrong.

JITTA. And you might forgive him. Very well: I give you leave to tell him. But you understand that if you tell him you must marry him; for you mustnt tell anyone except your husband.

EDITH. You want me to marry him?

JITTA. I do.

EDITH. Then I'll telephone him. I suppose that will do. I am so happy now that it doesnt matter tuppence whom I marry. [*Lenkheim opens the study door and is coming in when Edith, not hearing him, goes on*] I'd marry anyone to please you. I'd even marry Alfred.

LENKHEIM. Thank you. [*The two women spring up in dismay*]. Thats very kind of you, Edith, and very kind of Jitta to include me in the number of husbands she has apparently been offering you. But I have no intention of divorcing her at present.

EDITH [*not knowing what else to say*] It wasnt that. Mrs Lenkheim never offered you to me.

JITTA. Go off to the telephone, dear, and make it up with your man. I will make it up for you with Alfred.

LENKHEIM. Do, Edith. [*He crosses the room to the other door, and opens it for her with sardonic politeness*].

EDITH [*to Lenkheim, after kissing Jitta rather defiantly*] Mrs Lenkheim did not say a single unkind word about you. I did. [*She nods mockingly in his face and goes out*].

LENKHEIM. Have you told her?

JITTA [*her bored manner with her husband contrasting strongly with her warm interest in Edith*] She guessed. She knew. It is no use keeping secrets when they will not keep themselves. I have made her happy: that is all I care about. [*She goes listlessly to the window-seat, and sits there looking out, with her shoulder turned to him*].

LENKHEIM. And have you told the old woman? Have you made her happy?

JITTA. I have made her happy. But I did not tell her. The strange thing is that she guesses it too; but she will never know it. She doesnt want to know it. Edith did. That makes all the difference. I have made them both happy. I wish someone could make me happy.

LENKHEIM. As I unfortunately am only your husband, I suppose there is no use my trying.

JITTA [*turning her face to him with open contempt*] You!

LENKHEIM. Funny, isnt it?

JITTA [*rising*] Dont be insufferable. You owe it to your position as an injured husband never to speak to me when we are alone and there are no appearances to be kept up. You swore not to. And you have been talking to me ever since, except when there was somebody else present to talk to.

LENKHEIM. Make no mistake, Jitta: when I swore that, I meant it.

JITTA [*ironically*] So it appears.

72

LENKHEIM. When you swore to be faithful to me, you meant it, didnt you?

JITTA [*interrupting him curtly*] You need not remind me of that again. I have not denied it. I have not excused myself. But I do not intend to have it thrown in my teeth every time we meet. [*She turns away from him determinedly, and sits down in the chair between the table and the door*].

LENKHEIM. Very well, then, dont you start reminding me every time we meet that I swore to do a good many things that I find I cant do. Is that a bargain?

JITTA [*a little ashamed, feeling that she has allowed herself to descend to his level*] Yes. I beg your pardon. I should not have said it. But please remember that you can hurt me more than I can hurt you, because you have done nothing wrong. You are within your rights: you are above reproach: you have the superior position morally: no taunts of mine can degrade you as your reproaches can degrade me. [*Tragically*] I am a miserable creature. I betrayed you to please myself. I deserted him in his extremity to save myself. Please leave me to my disgrace. Nothing that you can say or think can add to the contempt I feel for myself.

LENKHEIM [*chuckling a little*] How you enjoy being miserable, Jitta!

JITTA. Enjoy!!

LENKHEIM. You just revel in it. You think yourself such a jolly romantic figure. You think that everything that happens to you is extraordinarily interesting because it happens to you. And you think that everything that happens to me is quite uninteresting because it hasnt happened to you. But what has happened to you has happened to lots of women—except, of course, the way it ended. And even that was an accident that might have happened to anyone.

JITTA. No doubt. Unfortunately, I did not behave as any decent woman would.

LENKHEIM. That is just where you are mistaken, darling. When you were brought to the point and put to the proof, you didnt

73

behave romantically: you behaved very sensibly. You kept your head, and did just the right thing. You saved your reputation and my reputation. You prevented a horrible scandal. You have managed to make his wife and daughter happy. And yet you think you are ashamed of yourself because you were not found stretched on his dead body, with the limelight streaming on your white face, and the band playing slow music.

JITTA. Oh, what a nature you have, Alfred! You are prosaic to the core.

LENKHEIM [*grinning*] If you had only been clever enough to take me in, your success would have been complete. It wouldnt have been difficult. I always took you in when I had an adventure.

JITTA [*rising, very unpleasantly surprised, and not a little furious*] You! You have had adventures since we were married? You have deceived me?

LENKHEIM. Now dont begin imagining that I am a Don Juan. To be precise, I have kissed other women twice. I was drunk both times. And I had a serious affair with your dear friend Thelma Petersen. That lasted until she and her husband went back to Norway.

JITTA. Oh, how disgraceful! And you call her my friend!

LENKHEIM. I call Bruno Haldenstedt my friend. So you see I am not your moral superior. I thought it might restore your happiness a little to know that.

JITTA. Alfred: I will never speak to you nor cross the threshold of your house again.

LENKHEIM [*more amused than ever*] Except when you call to tell me so. When you let out about Haldenstedt I felt just as you feel now. Tomorrow you will think better of it, as I have thought better of it.

JITTA [*more dignified than ever*] If you imagine that any relations that could exist between Mrs Petersen and yourself were in the least like my relations with Bruno, you only shew for the thousandth time how incapable you are of understanding either him or me.

LENKHEIM. I'm afraid you dont understand either Thelma or me as sympathetically as I could wish. Thelma was a very superior woman, let me tell you. If my taste did not lie in the direction of superior women I shouldnt have married you.

JITTA. I will not have it, Alfred. I will not be dragged down to your level.

LENKHEIM. Five minutes ago you were amusing yourself by pretending that you were beneath contempt.

JITTA. So I am, on my own plane, and on his. But not on yours.

LENKHEIM. I dont believe theres a woman alive who doesnt look on herself as a special creation, and consider her husband an inferior and common sort of animal.

JITTA. You forget that I did not think of Bruno in that way.

LENKHEIM. Yes; but then he wasnt your husband. Thelma thought me a much finer fellow than Petersen.

JITTA [*exasperated*] If you mention that woman to me again, I will break my promise to you, and walk straight out of your house before all the world.

LENKHEIM. That will only make us quits, because, as it happens, I am going to break my promise to you.

JITTA. How?

LENKHEIM. About the book. I have read it.

JITTA. Well?

LENKHEIM. Well, I'll be hanged if I put my name to it. In the first place nobody would believe I had ever written it. In the second, it's the most utter tommy-rot that was ever put forward as a serious contribution to psychology. Why, it flatly contradicts everything I have been teaching for years past, and everything I was taught myself.

JITTA [*intensely angry*] Does that prove it to be tommy-rot, or does it prove that you are an idiot?

LENKHEIM. I may be an idiot; but my idiocy is the accepted idiocy taught in the University at which I am a professor; and his idiocy is not taught anywhere. Do you forget that I have to earn bread for the household, and that your own money hardly pays for your dresses? This book would ruin us both.

JITTA. It is a sacred trust; and I swore to him that it should be fulfilled.

LENKHEIM. *I* didnt. And the old woman has just told me that he said the book was to be her insurance policy. No doubt I am Bruno's inferior; but I draw the line at helping him to rob his widow for my own profit.

JITTA. Then you refuse to carry out his intentions?

LENKHEIM. I cant carry out his intentions.

JITTA. You mean you wont.

LENKHEIM. I mean what I say. When he left me this book of his, he did so on the understanding that I was to know nothing of his relations with you. He hadnt quite such a low opinion of me as to suppose that I would take it as the price of my wife. Well, whose fault is it that I know all about it? Who let the secret out? You did.

JITTA [*collapsing into his chair*] Oh, how shamefully I have betrayed him at every step! How despicable I am!

LENKHEIM [*sympathetically*] Not a bit of it, dear. You have just said yourself that if secrets dont keep themselves, nobody can keep them. This secret wouldnt keep itself. Come! stop crying. If only you would be content to be a woman for a moment, and not a heroine! And oh Lord! if you only had the smallest sense of humor!

JITTA [*passionately*] You cant even try to console me without sneering at me. Do you know what Edith called you?

LENKHEIM. No. You can tell me if it will relieve your feelings.

JITTA. She said you were a chump; and so you are.

LENKHEIM. All husbands are chumps, dear, after the first month or so. Jolly good thing for their wives too, sometimes.

JITTA. What are you going to do with that book?

LENKHEIM. If I had any regard for his reputation I should burn it at our domestic hearth.

JITTA [*recovering her dignity; rising; and speaking with tranquil conviction*] You shall not do that, Alfred.

LENKHEIM. Perhaps not; but it would serve you right if I did.

JITTA. It would not serve Edith right. Besides, his work, his reputation, his greatness—for whatever you may say I know that that book is the greatest that ever was written—belong not only to humanity, but to her. And I love her as if she were my own daughter. I have no other child.

LENKHEIM [*wincing a little*] My fault, I suppose. Oh, you can be nasty when you want to, Jitta.

JITTA. Oh, no, no. Will you never understand?

LENKHEIM. Probably not, being only a chump. Be a little amiable, Jitta: I havnt been so very hard on you, have I?

JITTA [*insisting*] You will not destroy the book? You will edit it? You will do everything for it that you could for a book of your own?

LENKHEIM. Well, if—

Fessler and Edith come in arm-in-arm, followed by Mrs Haldenstedt.

EDITH. Here he is. Kiss him.

FESSLER [*hastily*] Tchut! [*Taking Jitta's hand, and kissing it*] I owe you my life's happiness, Mrs Lenkheim.

AGNES. I am sure we all owe you the happiness of our lives. You are our good angel: indeed you are. Oh, you are a lucky man, Mr Lenkheim, to have such a wife.

JITTA [*striking in before he can reply*] I have one more piece of news for you, Mrs Haldenstedt. Alfred has found your husband's book. It is a masterpiece. He will edit it. He will do everything he could do for it if it were his own book.

FESSLER [*triumphant*] Splendid!

AGNES [*overjoyed*] Oh, think of that! Edith [*she kisses Edith*]! Doctor [*she kisses the doctor*]! Professor [*she kisses Lenkheim*]! Didnt I say she was our good angel?

LENKHEIM. And now, may I take my good angel home?

AGNES [*to Jitta*] Oh, must you go, dear?

JITTA [*sweetly, to Agnes*] Yes, dear. [*Threateningly to Alfred*] Come home. [*She goes to the door*].

LENKHEIM [*cheerily, as he shakes hands with everybody*] Goodbye.

ALL [*shaking hands*] Goodbye. Goodbye. Goodbye.

JITTA [*sternly*] Alfred: come home.

LENKHEIM [*hastily obeying*] Yes, dear.

AGNES [*as the door closes sharply behind them*] She's too good for him.

TRIFLES AND TOMFOOLERIES

TRIFLES AND TOMFOOLERIES

All playwrights and all actors tomfool sometimes if they can. The practice needs no apology if it amuses them and their audiences harmlessly. Irresponsible laughter is salutary in small quantities. One throws off these things as Beethoven threw off a few bagatelles, and Mozart a few senseless bravura pieces for friends who were violinists. Besides, tomfoolery is as classic as tragedy. High comedy seldom achieves a whole act without revealing traces of its origin in the altercations and topical discussions of the circus clown with the ringmaster: what else indeed are the passages between Monsieur Jourdain and his philosophers and fencing masters in Molière's most famous comedy? I could cite many examples from plays of my own which pretend to be highly serious. The following playlets are tomfooleries pure and simple, except the tragedietta, which is only a trifle. I do not mean that their words are utterly void of wit and wisdom, or their figures characterless; for this kind of work would be unbearable if it added deficiency to folly. I mean just what I say: they are tomfooleries.

On their topical side they are more or less out of date; but as the world continues to excite itself over the same sort of scandal they can always be adapted to the cries of the moment. They may disgust the admirers of my more pretentious work; but these highbrows must remember that there is a demand for little things as well as for big things, and that as I happen to have a few little things in my shop I may as well put them in the window with the rest.

AYOT ST LAWRENCE, *July* 1926.

THE ADMIRABLE BASHVILLE

OR

CONSTANCY UNREWARDED

BEING THE NOVEL OF CASHEL BYRON'S
PROFESSION DONE INTO A STAGE PLAY
IN THREE ACTS AND IN BLANK VERSE

PREFACE

It may be asked why I wrote The Admirable Bashville in blank verse. My answer is that the operation of the copyright law of that time (now happily superseded) left me only a week to write it in. Blank verse is so childishly easy and expeditious (hence, by the way, Shakespear's copious output), that by adopting it I was enabled to do within the week what would have cost me a month in prose.

Besides, I am fond of blank verse. Not nineteenth century blank verse, of course, nor indeed, with a very few exceptions, any post-Shakespearean blank verse. Nay, not Shakespearean blank verse itself later than the histories. I am quite sure that anyone who is to recover the charm of blank verse must go back frankly to its beginnings, and start a literary pre-Raphaelite Brotherhood. I like the melodious sing-song, the clear simple one-line and two-line sayings, and the occasional rhymed tags, like the half closes in an eighteenth century symphony, in Peele, Kyd, Greene, and the histories of Shakespear. Accordingly, I poetasted The Admirable Bashville in the primitive Elizabethan style. And lest the literary connoisseurs should declare that there was not a single correct line in all my three acts, I stole or paraphrased a few from Marlowe and Shakespear (not to mention Henry Carey); so that if any man dared quote me derisively, he should do so in peril of inadvertently lighting on a purple patch from Hamlet or Faustus.

I also endeavored in this little play to prove that I was not the heartless creature some of my critics took me for. I observed the established laws of stage popularity and probability. I simplified the character of the heroine, and summed up her sweetness in the one sacred word: Love. I gave consistency to the heroism of Cashel. I paid to Morality, in the final scene, the tribute of poetic justice. I restored to Patriotism its usual place on the stage, and gracefully acknowledged The Throne as the fountain of social honor. I paid particular attention to the con-

struction of the play, which will be found equal in this respect
to the best contemporary models.

And the result was that the British playgoer, to whom Elizabethan English is a dead language, only half understood nine-
tenths of the play, and applauded the other tenth (the big
speeches) with a seriousness that was far funnier than any
burlesque.

The play, by the way, should be performed on an Elizabethan
stage, with traverses for the indoor scenes, and with only one
interval after the second act.

*   *   *   *   *   *

On reading over the above after a lapse of thirty years I am
not quite so sure as I was that Elizabethan English may not again
become a living language to the ordinary playgoer. To people
who never read anything but newspapers and popular magazines,
a good deal of Shakespear's more euphuistic blank verse is
hardly more intelligible than classical Greek. Even actors may
be heard repeating it by rote with an air that persuades the public
that they understand what they are saying; but it cannot impose
any such illusion on a professionally skilled listener.

Then there are the people who do not go to Protestant
churches nor read anything at all, and consequently understand
no English except modern vernacular English. This class is by
no means a negligible one even in the theatre; for it includes a
large body of intelligent manual and open air workers and sports-
men who, though after their day's exertions they fall asleep in
less than a minute if they sit down with an open book in their
hands, can be kept awake and alert very effectually in the theatre
by a play. Only, it must be a play in the vernacular. Otherwise
it does not exist for them except as an incomprehensible bore.

There was a time when not only the theatres but the news-
papers addressed themselves to the literate alone. Hunt up an
old melodrama (say Sweeny Todd the Demon Barber of Fleet
Street) or an old newspaper file; and you will at once see that the
writers of the play and of the contemporary leading articles,
though they may have been the seediest of Bohemians, had learnt

Latin grammar and read books written by persons similarly schooled. They had literally the benefit of clergy, and wrote accordingly. With the advent of compulsory education sixty years ago, and the creation thereby of a class which could read and write, but had no Latin and less Greek, newspapers and plays alike soon came to be written by illiterate masters of the vernacular; and I myself welcomed the change and discarded my early very classical style for a vernacular one. Nowadays, when I read typewritten plays by young authors, as I sometimes have occasion to do, I find in them such illiteracies as He exits, She exits, They exit etc. etc. Chapman, who wrote all his stage directions in Latin, or Ben Jonson, who deplored the slenderness of Shakespear's classical education, would have risen up and roared for a birchrod to castigate such execrable solecisms. By the end of the nineteenth century the press and the theatre had lost all their Latinity; and this was why, whenever The Admirable Bashville was performed, men of letters like Maurice Hewlett would chuckle delightedly over it almost line by line, whilst the ordinary playgoers would listen with a puzzled and troubled stare, wondering what on earth it was all about and how they ought to take it, and the unfortunate persons who had been forced to "get up Shakespear" as part of an academic course on English literature, sat with a scowl of malignant hatred that poisoned the atmosphere. When Bashville was followed by a piece in the vernacular the relief of the audience was so great that there was always a burst of applause at the very first sentence.

And yet, whenever the meaning of the words was clear, the listeners shewed unmistakably that they liked hyperbolical rhetoric and deliberately artificial language. My parodies of the Elizabethan mannerism, and funny echoes of pet lines from the Elizabethan playwrights were, as such, quite lost on them; but Ben Webster brought down the house with Cashel Byron's declamatory repudiation of the name of gentleman, and James Hearn's lamentation over the tragedy of Cetewayo came off, not as a mockery, but as genuine tragedy, which indeed it also is. It was the literary fun that proved a mere puzzle, in spite of the acting of casts which included such accomplished comedians as Charles Quatermaine, William Wyes, Lennox Pawle, Henrietta Watson, Marie Lohr, and Fanny Brough.

Another significant fact pointed in the same direction. In no country is the worship of the old authorized version of the Bible carried to greater lengths than in the United States of America. To alter a single word of it was, it was believed, to incur the curse in the last chapter of Revelations. Even in England the very timid official revision of 1885 shocked our native Fundamentalists (a ridiculous but convenient name not then invented). Yet it was in the United States that the ministers of religion first found themselves compelled to produce versions in modern vernacular and journalese under stress of the flat fact that their flocks often could not understand the old authorized version, and always found the style so artificial that though it could produce an unintelligent reverence it brought no intimate conviction to the reader.

Sometimes, however, the simple and direct passages were not sentimental enough to satisfy people whose minds were steeped in modern literary sob stuff. For instance, such bald statements about Barabbas as that he was a robber, or that he had killed a certain man in a sedition, quite failed to interest anyone in him; but when Marie Corelli expanded this concise information into a novel in her own passionate and richly colored style it sold like hot cakes.

I must make a personal confession in this matter. Though I was saturated with the Bible and with Shakespear before I was ten years old, and the only grammar I ever learned was Latin grammar, so that Elizabethan English became a mother tongue to me, yet when I first read such vivid and unaffected modern versions as Dr James Moffatt's New Translation of the New Testament I at once got from them so many lights on the Bible narratives which I had missed in the authorized version that I said to myself "Some day I will translate Hamlet into modern vernacular English." But indeed if the alienation of our young from Elizabethan English continues it will be necessary to pro-

duce revised versions not only of Shakespear but of Sir Walter
Scott and even of my own early novels.

Still, a revival of Elizabethan literature may be possible. If I,
as an Irish child in the eighteen-sixties, could without enforced
study become so familiar with it that I had some difficulty as a
journalist later on in getting rid of it, it must be possible for the
same thing to occur to an English child in the nineteen-sixties.
The Elizabethan style has many charms for imaginative children.
It is bloody, bombastic, violent, senselessly pretentious, barbarous and childish in its humor, and full of music. In short, the
taste for it, as anyone can observe at the Old Vic or the Stratford
Festivals, is essentially half childish, half musical. To acquire it,
all that is necessary is access to it. Now the opportunities for
such access are enormously wider than they used to be. Of course
as long as we persist in stuffing Shakespear and the Bible down
our children's throats with threats of condign punishment if they
fail to answer silly questions about them, they will continue to
be loathed as they very largely are at present. But if our children,
when they have been simply taught to read, have plenty of dramatically illustrated Bibles and Shakespears left in their way, with
the illustrated passages printed under the pictures, it will soon
be possible to find a general audience which can laugh at The
Admirable Bashville as heartily as Maurice Hewlett did, and for
repertory theatres to amuse themselves and their congregations
with occasional performances of Carey's Chrononhotonthologos,
Fielding's Tom Thumb, and even Bombastes Furioso.

I shall not here raise the question of whether such a revival
is desirable. It would carry me too far and plunge me too deep
for a volume of trifles and tomfooleries. But as the Elizabethan
style is unquestionably both musical and powerful, I may at
least say that it is better to have a sense of it and a fancy for it
than to have no sense of style or literary fancy at all.

THE ADMIRABLE BASHVILLE; OR, CONSTANCY UNREWARDED

ACT I

A glade in Wiltstoken Park

Enter LYDIA

LYDIA. Ye leafy breasts and warm protecting wings
Of mother trees that hatch our tender souls,
And from the well of Nature in our hearts
Thaw the intolerable inch of ice
That bears the weight of all the stamping world,
Hear ye me sing to solitude that I,
Lydia Carew, the owner of these lands,
Albeit most rich, most learned, and most wise,
Am yet most lonely. What are riches worth
When wisdom with them comes to shew the purse bearer
That life remains unpurchasable? Learning
Learns but one lesson: doubt! To excel all
Is, to be lonely. Oh, ye busy birds,
Engrossed with real needs, ye shameless trees
With arms outspread in welcome of the sun,
Your minds, bent singly to enlarge your lives,
Have given you wings and raised your delicate heads
High heavens above us crawlers.

[*A rook sets up a great cawing; and the other birds chatter loudly
as a gust of wind sets the branches swaying. She makes as
though she would shew them her sleeves.*

Lo, the leaves
That hide my drooping boughs! Mock me—poor maid!—
Deride with joyous comfortable chatter
These stolen feathers. Laugh at me, the clothed one.
Laugh at the mind fed on foul air and books.
Books! Art! And Culture! Oh, I shall go mad.
Give me a mate that never heard of these,

A sylvan god, tree born in heart and sap;
Or else, eternal maidhood be my hap.

> [*Another gust of wind and bird-chatter. She sits on the mossy root of an oak and buries her face in her hands. Cashel Byron, in a white singlet and breeches, comes through the trees.*

CASHEL. Whats this? Whom have we here? A woman!

LYDIA [*looking up*]   Yes.

CASHEL. You have no business here. I have. Away!
Women distract me. Hence!

LYDIA.   Bid you me hence?
I am upon mine own ground. Who are you?
I take you for a god, a sylvan god.
This place is mine: I share it with the birds,
The trees, the sylvan gods, the lovely company
Of haunted solitudes.

CASHEL.   A sylvan god!
A goat-eared image! Do your statues speak?
Walk? heave the chest with breath? or like a feather
Lift you—like this?   [*He sets her on her feet.*

LYDIA [*panting*] You take away my breath!
Youre strong. Your hands off, please. Thank you. Farewell.

CASHEL. Before you go: when shall we meet again?

LYDIA. Why should we meet again?

CASHEL.   Who knows? We shall.
That much I know by instinct. Whats your name?

LYDIA. Lydia Carew.

CASHEL.   Lydia's a pretty name.
Where do you live?

LYDIA.   I' the castle.

CASHEL [*thunderstruck*]   Do not say
You are the lady of this great domain.

LYDIA. I am.

CASHEL.   Accursed luck! I took you for
The daughter of some farmer. Well, your pardon.
I came too close: I looked too deep. Farewell.

LYDIA. I pardon that. Now tell me who you are.

CASHEL. Ask me not whence I come, nor what I am.
You are the lady of the castle. I
Have but this hard and blackened hand to live by.

LYDIA. I have felt its strength and envied you. Your name?
I have told you mine.

CASHEL.   My name is Cashel Byron.

LYDIA. I never heard the name; and yet you utter it
As men announce a celebrated name.
Forgive my ignorance.

CASHEL.   I bless it, Lydia.
I have forgot your other name.

LYDIA.   Carew.
Cashel's a pretty name too.

MELLISH [*calling through the wood*] Coo-ee! Byron!

CASHEL. A thousand curses! Oh, I beg you, go.
This is a man you must not meet.

MELLISH [*further off*]   Coo-ee!

LYDIA. He's losing us. What does he in my woods?

CASHEL. He is a part of what I am. What that is
You must not know. It would end all between us.
And yet there's no dishonor in't: your lawyer,
Who let your lodge to me, will vouch me honest.
I am ashamed to tell you what I am—
At least, as yet. Some day, perhaps.

MELLISH [*nearer*]   Coo-ee!

LYDIA. His voice is nearer. Fare you well, my tenant.
When next your rent falls due, come to the castle.
Pay me in person. Sir: your most obedient.

                            [*She curtsies and goes*

CASHEL. Lives in this castle! Owns this park! A lady
Marry a prizefighter! Impossible.
And yet the prizefighter must marry her.

Enter MELLISH

Ensanguined swine, whelped by a doggish dam,
Is this thy park, that thou, with voice obscene,

Fillst it with yodeled yells, and screamst my name
For all the world to know that Cashel Byron
Is training here for combat.

MELLISH. Swine you me?
Ive caught you, have I? You have found a woman.
Let her shew here again, I'll set the dog on her.
I will. I say it. And my name's Bob Mellish.

CASHEL. Change thy initial and be truly hight
Hellish. As for thy dog, why dost thou keep one
And bark thyself? Begone.

MELLISH. I'll not begone.
You shall come back with me and do your duty—
Your duty to your backers, do you hear?
You have not punched the bag this bléssed day.

CASHEL. The putrid bag engirdled by thy belt
Invites my fist.

MELLISH [weeping] Ingrate! O wretched lot!
Who would a trainer be? O Mellish, Mellish,
Trainer of heroes, builder-up of brawn,
Vicarious victor, thou createst champions
That quickly turn thy tyrants. But beware:
Without me thou art nothing. Disobey me,
And all thy boasted strength shall fall from thee.
With flaccid muscles and with failing breath
Facing the fist of thy more faithful foe,
I'll see thee on the grass cursing the day
Thou didst forswear thy training.

CASHEL. Noisome quack
That canst not from thine own abhorrent visage
Take one carbuncle, thou contaminat'st
Even with thy presence my untainted blood.
Preach abstinence to rascals like thyself
Rotten with surfeiting. Leave me in peace.
This grove is sacred: thou profanest it.
Hence! I have business that concerns thee not.

MELLISH. Ay, with your woman. You will lose your fight.

Have you forgot your duty to your backers?
Oh, what a sacred thing your duty is!
What makes a man but duty? Where were we
Without our duty? Think of Nelson's words:
England expects that every man—

CASHEL.   Shall twaddle
About his duty. Mellish: at no hour
Can I regard thee wholly without loathing;
But when thou playst the moralist, by Heaven,
My soul flies to my fist, my fist to thee;
And never did the Cyclops' hammer fall
On Mars's armor—but enough of that.
It does remind me of my mother.

MELLISH.   Ah,
Byron, let it remind thee. Once I heard
An old song: it ran thus. [*He clears his throat*] Ahem, Ahem!
    [*Sings*]—They say there is no other
                Can take the place of mother—
I am out o' voice: forgive me; but remember:
Thy mother—were that sainted woman here—
Would say, Obey thy trainer.

CASHEL.   Now, by Heaven,
Some fate is pushing thee upon thy doom.
Canst thou not hear thy sands as they run out?
They thunder like an avalanche. Old man:
Two things I hate, my duty and my mother.
Why dost thou urge them both upon me now?
Presume not on thine age and on thy nastiness.
Vanish, and promptly.

MELLISH.   Can I leave thee here
Thus thinly clad, exposed to vernal dews?
Come back with me, my son, unto our lodge.

CASHEL. Within this breast a fire is newly lit
Whose glow shall sun the dew away, whose radiance
Shall make the orb of night hang in the heavens
Unnoticed, like a glow-worm at high noon.

MELLISH. Ah me, ah me, where wilt thou spend the night?

CASHEL. Wiltstoken's windows wandering beneath,
Wiltstoken's holy bell hearkening,
Wiltstoken's lady loving breathlessly.

MELLISH. The lady of the castle! Thou art mad.

CASHEL. Tis thou art mad to trifle in my path.
Thwart me no more. Begone.

MELLISH.   My boy, my son,
I'd give my heart's blood for thy happiness.
Thwart thee, my son! Ah no. I'll go with thee.
I'll brave the dews. I'll sacrifice my sleep.
I am old—no matter: ne'er shall it be said
Mellish deserted thee.

CASHEL.   You resolute gods
That will not spare this man, upon your knees
Take the disparity twixt his age and mine.
Now from the ring to the high judgment seat
I step at your behest. Bear you me witness
This is not Victory, but Execution.

> [*He solemnly projects his fist with colossal force against the waist-
> coat of Mellish, who doubles up like a folded towel, and lies
> without sense or motion.*

And now the night is beautiful again.

> [*The castle clock strikes the hour in the distance.*

Hark! Hark! Hark! Hark! Hark! Hark! Hark! Hark! Hark!
    Hark!
It strikes in poetry. Tis ten o'clock.
Lydia: to thee!

> [*He steals off towards the castle. Mellish stirs and groans.*

ACT II

SCENE I

London. A room in Lydia's house

Enter LYDIA *and* LUCIAN

LYDIA. Welcome, dear cousin, to my London house.
Of late you have been chary of your visits.

LUCIAN. I have been greatly occupied of late.
The minister to whom I act as scribe
In Downing Street was born in Birmingham,
And, like a thoroughbred commercial statesman,
Splits his infinitives, which I, poor slave,
Must reunite, though all the time my heart
Yearns for my gentle coz's company.

LYDIA. Lucian: there is some other reason. Think!
Since England was a nation every mood
Her scribes with adverbs recklessly have split,
But thine avoidance dates from yestermonth.

LUCIAN. There is a man I like not haunts this house.

LYDIA. Thou speakst of Cashel Byron?

LUCIAN.   Aye, of him.
Hast thou forgotten that eventful night
When as we gathered were at Hoskyn House
To hear a lecture by Herr Abendgasse,
He placed a single finger on my chest,
And I, ensorceled, would have sunk supine
Had not a chair received my falling form.

LYDIA. Pooh! That was but by way of illustration.

LUCIAN. What right had he to illustrate his point
Upon my person? Was I his assistant
That he should try experiments on me
As Simpson did on his with chloroform?
Now, by the cannon balls of Galileo
He hath unmanned me: all my nerve is gone.

This very morning my official chief,
Tapping with friendly forefinger this button,
Levelled me like a thunderstricken elm
Flat upon the Colonial Office floor.

LYDIA. Fancies, coz.

LUCIAN.   Fancies! Fits! the chief said fits!
Delirium tremens! the chlorotic dance
Of Vitus! What could anyone have thought?
Your ruffian friend hath ruined me. By Heaven,
I tremble at a thumbnail. Give me drink.

LYDIA. What ho, without there! Bashville.

BASHVILLE [*without*]   Coming, madam.

Enter BASHVILLE

LYDIA. My cousin ails, Bashville. Procure some wet.

[*Exit* BASHVILLE.

LUCIAN. Some wet!!! Where learnt you that atrocious word?
This is the language of a flower-girl.

LYDIA. True. It is horrible. Said I "Some wet"?
I meant, some drink. Why did I say "Some wet"?
Am I ensorceled too? "Some wet"! Fie! fie!
I feel as though some hateful thing had stained me.
Oh, Lucian, how could I have said "Some wet"?

LUCIAN. The horrid conversation of this man
Hath numbed thy once unfailing sense of fitness.

LYDIA. Nay, he speaks very well: he's literate:
Shakespear he quotes unconsciously.

LUCIAN.   And yet
Anon he talks pure pothouse.

Enter BASHVILLE

BASHVILLE.   Sir: your potion.

LUCIAN. Thanks. [*He drinks*]. I am better.

A NEWSBOY [*calling without*]   Extra special Star!
Result of the great fight! Name of the winner!

LYDIA. Who calls so loud?

BASHVILLE. The papers, madam.

LYDIA. Why?
Hath ought momentous happened?

BASHVILLE. Madam: yes.
[*He produces a newspaper.*
All England for these thrilling paragraphs
A week has waited breathless.

LYDIA. Read them us.

BASHVILLE [*reading*] "At noon today, unknown to the police,
Within a thousand miles of Wormwood Scrubbs,
Th' Australian Champion and his challenger,
The Flying Dutchman, formerly engaged
I' the mercantile marine, fought to a finish.
Lord Worthington, the well-known sporting peer,
Was early on the scene."

LYDIA. Lord Worthington!

BASHVILLE. "The bold Ned Skene revisited the ropes
To hold the bottle for his quondam novice;
Whilst in the seaman's corner were assembled
Professor Palmer and the Chelsea Snob.
Mellish, whose epigastrium has been hurt,
Tis said, by accident at Wiltstoken,
Looked none the worse in the Australian's corner.
The Flying Dutchman wore the Union Jack:
His colors freely sold amid the crowd;
But Cashel's well-known spot of white on blue—"

LYDIA. Whose, did you say?

BASHVILLE. Cashel's, my lady.

LYDIA. Lucian:
Your hand—a chair—

BASHVILLE. Madam: youre ill.

LYDIA. Proceed.
What you have read I do not understand;
Yet I will hear it through. Proceed.

LUCIAN. Proceed.

BASHVILLE. "But Cashel's well-known spot of white on blue

99

Was fairly rushed for. Time was called at twelve,
When, with a smile of confidence upon
His ocean-beaten mug—"

LYDIA.   His mug?

LUCIAN [*explaining*]   His face.

BASHVILLE [*continuing*] "The Dutchman came undaunted to
   the scratch,
But found the champion there already. Both
Most heartily shook hands, amid the cheers
Of their encouraged backers. Two to one
Was offered on the Melbourne nonpareil;
And soon, so fit the Flying Dutchman seemed,
Found takers everywhere. No time was lost
In getting to the business of the day.
The Dutchman led at once, and seemed to land
On Byron's dicebox; but the seaman's reach,
Too short for execution at long shots,
Did not get fairly home upon the ivory;
And Byron had the best of the exchange."

LYDIA. I do not understand. What were they doing?

LUCIAN. Fighting with naked fists.

LYDIA.   Oh, horrible!
I'll hear no more. Or stay: how did it end?
Was Cashel hurt?

LUCIAN [*to Bashville*] Skip to the final round.

BASHVILLE. "Round Three: the rumors that had gone about
Of a breakdown in Byron's recent training
Seemed quite confirmed. Upon the call of time
He rose, and, looking anything but cheerful,
Proclaimed with every breath Bellows to Mend.
At this point six to one was freely offered
Upon the Dutchman; and Lord Worthington
Plunged at this figure till he stood to lose
A fortune should the Dutchman, as seemed certain,
Take down the number of the Panley boy.
The Dutchman, glutton as we know he is,

Seemed this time likely to go hungry. Cashel
Was clearly groggy as he slipped the sailor,
Who, not to be denied, followed him up,
Forcing the fighting mid tremendous cheers."

LYDIA. Oh stop—no more—or tell the worst at once.
I'll be revenged. Bashville: call the police.
This brutal sailor shall be made to know
There's law in England.

LUCIAN.   Do not interrupt him:
Mine ears are thirsting. Finish, man. What next?

BASHVILLE. "Forty to one, the Dutchman's friends exclaimed.
Done, said Lord Worthington, who shewed himself
A sportsman every inch. Barely the bet
Was booked, when, at the reeling champion's jaw
The sailor, bent on winning out of hand,
Sent in his right. The issue seemed a cert,
When Cashel, ducking smartly to his left,
Cross-countered like a hundredweight of brick—"

LUCIAN. Death and damnation!

LYDIA.   Oh, what does it mean?

BASHVILLE. "The Dutchman went to grass, a beaten man."

LYDIA. Hurrah! Hurrah! Hurrah! Oh, well done, Cashel!

BASHVILLE. "A scene of indescribable excitement
Ensued; for it was now quite evident
That Byron's grogginess had all along
Been feigned to make the market for his backers.
We trust this sample of colonial smartness
Will not find imitators on this side.
The losers settled up like gentlemen;
But many felt that Byron shewed bad taste
In taking old Ned Skene upon his back,
And, with Bob Mellish tucked beneath his oxter,
Sprinting a hundred yards to show the crowd
The perfect pink of his condition"—[a knock].

LYDIA [turning pale]   Bashville,
Didst hear? A knock.

BASHVILLE.   Madam: tis Byron's knock.
Shall I admit him?

LUCIAN.   Reeking from the ring!
Oh, monstrous! Say youre out.

LYDIA.   Send him away.
I will not see the wretch. How dare he keep
Secrets from ME? I'll punish him. Pray say
I'm not at home. [*Bashville turns to go*]. Yet stay. I am afraid
He will not come again.

LUCIAN.   A consummation
Devoutly to be wished by any lady.
Pray, do you wish this man to come again?

LYDIA. No, Lucian. He hath used me very ill.
He should have told me. I will ne'er forgive him.
Say, Not at home.

BASHVILLE.   Yes, madam.   [*Exit.*

LYDIA.   Stay—

LUCIAN [*stopping her*]   No, Lydia:
You shall not countermand that proper order.
Oh, would you cast the treasure of your mind,
The thousands at your bank, and, above all,
Your unassailable social position
Before this soulless mass of beef and brawn.

LYDIA Nay, coz: youre prejudiced.

CASHEL [*without*]   Liar and slave!

LYDIA. What words were those?

LUCIAN.   The man is drunk with slaughter.

Enter BASHVILLE *running: he shuts the door and locks it*

BASHVILLE. Save yourselves: at the staircase foot the champion
Sprawls on the mat, by trick of wrestler tripped;
But when he rises, woe betide us all!

LYDIA. Who bade you treat my visitor with violence?

BASHVILLE. He would not take my answer; thrust the door
Back in my face; gave me the lie i' th' throat;
Averred he felt your presence in his bones.

I said he should feel mine there too, and felled him;
Then fled to bar your door.

LYDIA.   O lover's instinct!
He felt my presence. Well, let him come in.
We must not fail in courage with a fighter.
Unlock the door.

LUCIAN.   Stop. Like all women, Lydia,
You have the courage of immunity.
To strike you were against his code of honor;
But me, above the belt, he may perform on
T' th' height of his profession. Also Bashville.

BASHVILLE. Think not of me, sir. Let him do his worst.
Oh, if the valor of my heart could weigh
The fatal difference twixt his weight and mine,
A second battle should he do this day:
Nay, though outmatched I be, let but my mistress
Give me the word: instant I'll take him on
Here—now—at catchweight. Better bite the carpet
A man, than fly, a coward.

LUCIAN.   Bravely said:
I will assist you with the poker.

LYDIA.   No:
I will not have him touched. Open the door.

BASHVILLE. Destruction knocks thereat. I smile, and open.
[*Bashville opens the door. Dead silence. Cashel enters, in tears.
A solemn pause.*

CASHEL. You know my secret?

LYDIA.   Yes.

CASHEL.   And thereupon
You bade your servant fling me from your door.

LYDIA. I bade my servant say I was not here.

CASHEL [*to Bashville*] Why didst thou better thy instruction,
    man?
Hadst thou but said, "She bade me tell thee this,"
Thoudst burst my heart. I thank thee for thy mercy.

LYDIA. Oh, Lucian, didst thou call him "drunk with slaughter"?

Canst thou refrain from weeping at his woe?

CASHEL [*to Lucian*] The unwritten law that shields the amateur
Against professional resentment, saves thee.
O coward, to traduce behind their backs
Defenceless prizefighters!

LUCIAN. Thou dost avow
Thou art a prizefighter.

CASHEL. It was my glory.
I had hoped to offer to my lady there
My belts, my championships, my heaped-up stakes,
My undefeated record; but I knew
Behind their blaze a hateful secret lurked.

LYDIA. Another secret?

LUCIAN. Is there worse to come?

CASHEL. Know ye not then my mother is an actress?

LUCIAN. How horrible!

LYDIA. Nay, nay: how interesting!

CASHEL. A thousand victories cannot wipe out
That birthstain. Oh, my speech bewrayeth it:
My earliest lesson was the player's speech
In Hamlet; and to this day I express myself
More like a mobled queen than like a man
Of flesh and blood. Well may your cousin sneer!
What's Hecuba to him or he to Hecuba?

LUCIAN. Injurious upstart: if by Hecuba
Thou pointest darkly at my lovely cousin,
Know that she is to me, and I to her,
What never canst thou be. I do defy thee;
And maugre all the odds thy skill doth give,
Outside I will await thee.

LYDIA. I forbid
Expressly any such duello. Bashville:
The door. Put Mr Webber in a hansom,
And bid the driver hie to Downing Street.
No answer: tis my will. [*Exeunt* LUCIAN *and* BASHVILLE.
And now, farewell.

You must not come again, unless indeed
You can some day look in my eyes and say:
Lydia: my occupation's gone.

CASHEL.   Ah no:
It would remind you of my wretched mother.
O God, let me be natural a moment!
What other occupation can I try?
What would you have me be?

LYDIA.   A gentleman.

CASHEL. A gentleman! Cashel Byron, stoop
To be the thing that bets on me! the fool
I flatter at so many coins a lesson!
The screaming creature who beside the ring
Gambles with basest wretches for my blood,
And pays with money that he never earned!
Let me die broken hearted rather!

LYDIA.   But
You need not be an idle gentleman.
I call you one of Nature's gentlemen.

CASHEL. Thats the collection for the loser, Lydia.
I am not wont to need it. When your friends
Contest elections, and at foot o' th' poll
Rue their presumption, tis their wont to claim
A moral victory. In a sort they are
Nature's M.P.s. I am not yet so threadbare
As to accept these consolation stakes.

LYDIA. You are offended with me.

CASHEL.   Yes I am.
I can put up with much; but—"Nature's gentleman"!
I thank your ladyship of Lyons, but
Must beg to be excused.

LYDIA.   But surely, surely,
To be a prizefighter, and maul poor mariners
With naked knuckles, is no work for you.

CASHEL. Thou dost arraign the inattentive Fates
That weave my thread of life in ruder patterns

105

Than these that lie, antimacassarly,
Asprent thy drawing room. As well demand
Why I at birth chose to begin my life
A speechless babe, hairless, incontinent,
Hobbling upon all fours, a nurse's nuisance?
Or why I do propose to lose my strength,
To blanch my hair, to let the gums recede
Far up my yellowing teeth, and finally
Lie down and moulder in a rotten grave?
Only one thing more foolish could have been,
And that was to be born, not man, but woman.
This was thy folly, why rebuk'st thou mine?

    LYDIA. These are not things of choice.

    CASHEL.   And did I choose
My quick divining eye, my lightning hand,
My springing muscle and untiring heart?
Did I implant the instinct in the race
That found a use for these, and said to me,
Fight for us, and be fame and fortune thine?

    LYDIA. But there are other callings in the world.

    CASHEL. Go tell thy painters to turn stockbrokers,
Thy poet friends to stoop oer merchants' desks
And pen prose records of the gains of greed.
Tell bishops that religion is outworn,
And that the Pampa to the horsebreaker
Opes new careers. Bid the professor quit
His fraudulent pedantries, and do i' the world
The thing he would teach others. Then return
To me and say: Cashel: they have obeyed;
And on that pyre of sacrifice I, too,
Will throw my championship.

    LYDIA.   But tis so cruel.

    CASHEL. Is it so? I have hardly noticed that,
So cruel are all callings. Yet this hand,
That many a two days bruise hath ruthless given,
Hath kept no dungeon locked for twenty years,

Hath slain no sentient creature for my sport.
I am too squeamish for your dainty world,
That cowers behind the gallows and the lash,
The world that robs the poor, and with their spoil
Does what its tradesmen tell it. Oh, your ladies!
Sealskinned and egret-feathered; all defiance
To Nature; cowering if one say to them
"What will the servants think?" Your gentlemen!
Your tailor-tyrannized visitors of whom
Flutter of wing and singing in the wood
Make chickenbutchers. And your medicine men!
Groping for cures in the tormented entrails
Of friendly dogs. Pray have you asked all these
To change their occupations? Find you mine
So grimly crueller? I cannot breathe
An air so petty and so poisonous.

    LYDIA. But find you not their manners very nice?

    CASHEL. To me, perfection. Oh, they condescend
With a rare grace. Your duke, who condescends
Almost to the whole world, might for a Man
Pass in the eyes of those who never saw
The duke capped with a prince. See then, ye gods,
The duke turn footman, and his eager dame
Sink the great lady in the obsequious housemaid!
Oh, at such moments I could wish the Court
Had but one breadbasket, that with my fist
I could make all its windy vanity
Gasp itself out on the gravel. Fare you well.
I did not choose my calling; but at least
I can refrain from being a gentleman.

    LYDIA. You say farewell to me without a pang.

    CASHEL. My calling hath apprenticed me to pangs.
This is a rib-bender; but I can bear it.
It is a lonely thing to be a champion.

    LYDIA. It is a lonelier thing to be a woman.

    CASHEL. Be lonely then. Shall it be said of thee

That for his brawn thou misalliance mad'st
Wi' the Prince of Ruffians? Never. Go thy ways;
Or, if thou hast nostalgia of the mud,
Wed some bedoggéd wretch that on the slot
Of gilded snobbery, *ventre à terre*,
Will hunt through life with eager nose on earth
And hang thee thick with diamonds. I am rich;
But all my gold was fought for with my hands.

    LYDIA. What dost thou mean by rich?

    CASHEL.   There is a man,
Hight Paradise, vaunted unconquerable,
Hath dared to say he will be glad to hear from me.
I have replied that none can hear from me
Until a thousand solid pounds be staked.
His friends have confidently found the money.
Ere fall of leaf that money shall be mine;
And then I shall possess ten thousand pounds.
I had hoped to tempt thee with that monstrous sum.

    LYDIA. Thou silly Cashel, tis but a week's income.
I did propose to give thee three times that
For pocket money when we two were wed.

    CASHEL. Give me my hat. I have been fooling here.
Now, by the Hebrew lawgiver, I thought
That only in America such revenues
Were decent deemed. Enough. My dream is dreamed.
Your gold weighs like a mountain on my chest.
Farewell.

    LYDIA. The golden mountain shall be thine
The day thou quitst thy horrible profession.

    CASHEL. Tempt me not, woman. It is honor calls.
Slave to the Ring I rest until the face
Of Paradise be changed.

Enter BASHVILLE

    BASHVILLE.   Madam, your carriage,
Ordered by you at two. Tis now half-past.

CASHEL. Sdeath! is it half-past two? The king! the king!

LYDIA. The king! What mean you?

CASHEL.   I must meet a monarch
This very afternoon at Islington.

LYDIA. At Islington! You must be mad.

CASHEL.   A cab!
Go call a cab; and let a cab be called;
And let the man that calls it be thy footman.

LYDIA. You are not well. You shall not go alone.
My carriage waits. I must accompany you.
I go to find my hat.   [*Exit.*

CASHEL.   Like Paracelsus,
Who went to find his soul [*To Bashville*] And now, young man,
How comes it that a fellow of your inches,
So deft a wrestler and so bold a spirit,
Can stoop to be a flunkey? Call on me
On your next evening out. I'll make a man of you.
Surely you are ambitious and aspire—

BASHVILLE. To be a butler and draw corks; wherefore,
By Heaven, I will draw yours.
                    [*He hits Cashel on the nose, and runs out.*
CASHEL [*thoughtfully putting the side of his forefinger to his nose,
and studying the blood on it*] Too quick for me!
There's money in this youth.

Re-enter LYDIA, *hatted and gloved*

LYDIA.   O Heaven! you bleed.

CASHEL. Lend me a key or other frigid object,
That I may put it down my back, and staunch
The welling life stream.

LYDIA [*giving him her keys*] Oh, what have you done?

CASHEL. Flush on the boko napped your footman's left.

LYDIA. I do not understand.

CASHEL.   True. Pardon me.
I have received a blow upon the nose
In sport from Bashville. Next, ablution; else

I shall be total gules.   *[He hurries out.*

    LYDIA.   How well he speaks!
There is a silver trumpet in his lips
That stirs me to the finger ends. His nose
Dropt lovely color: tis a perfect blood.
I would twere mingled with mine own!

Enter BASHVILLE

                     What now?

    BASHVILLE. Madam, the coachman can no longer wait:
The horses will take cold.

    LYDIA.   I do beseech him
A moment's grace. Oh, mockery of wealth!
The third class passenger unchidden rides
Whither and when he will: obsequious trams
Await him hourly: subterranean tubes
With tireless coursers whisk him through the town;
But we, the rich, are slaves to Houyhnhnms:
We wait upon their colds, and frowst all day
Indoors, if they but cough or spurn their hay.

    BASHVILLE. Madam, an omnibus to Euston Road,
And thence t' th' Angel—

Enter CASHEL

    LYDIA.   Let us haste, my love:
The coachman is impatient.

    CASHEL.   Did he guess
He stays for Cashel Byron, he'd outwait
Pompei's sentinel. Let us away.
This day of deeds, as yet but half begun,
Must ended be in merrie Islington.

                  [Exeunt LYDIA *and* CASHEL.

    BASHVILLE. Gods! how she hangs on's arm! I am alone.
Now let me lift the cover from my soul.
O wasted humbleness! Deluded diffidence!
How often have I said, Lie down, poor footman:

OR, CONSTANCY UNREWARDED

She'll never stoop to thee, rear as thou wilt
Thy powder to the sky. And now, by Heaven,
She stoops below me; condescends upon
This hero of the pothouse, whose exploits,
Writ in my character from my last place,
Would damn me into ostlerdom. And yet
Theres an eternal justice in it; for
By so much as the ne'er subduéd Indian
Excels the servile negro, doth this ruffian
Precedence take of me. "*Ich dien.*" Damnation!
I serve. My motto should have been, "I scalp."
And yet I do not bear the yoke for gold.
Because I love her I have blacked her boots;
Because I love her I have cleaned her knives,
Doing in this the office of a boy,
Whilst, like the celebrated maid that milks
And does the meanest chares, Ive shared the passions
Of Cleopatra. It has been my pride
To give her place the greater altitude
By lowering mine, and of her dignity
To be so jealous that my cheek has flamed
Even at the thought of such a deep disgrace
As love for such a one as I would be
For such a one as she; and now! and now!
A prizefighter! O irony! O bathos!
To have made way for this! Oh, Bashville, Bashville:
Why hast thou thought so lowly of thyself,
So heavenly high of her? Let what will come,
My love must speak: twas my respect was dumb.

III

SCENE II

*The Agricultural Hall in Islington, crowded with spectators. In the
arena a throne, with a boxing ring before it. A balcony above
on the right, occupied by persons of fashion: among others,
Lydia and Lord Worthington.*

Flourish. Enter LUCIAN *and* CETEWAYO, *with Chiefs
in attendance*

CETEWAYO. Is this the Hall of Husbandmen?

LUCIAN.   It is.

CETEWAYO. Are these anæmic dogs the English people?

LUCIAN. Mislike us not for our complexions,
The pallied liveries of the pall of smoke
Belched by the mighty chimneys of our factories,
And by the million patent kitchen ranges
Of happy English homes.

CETEWAYO.   When first I came
I deemed those chimneys the fuliginous altars
Of some infernal god. I now perceive
The English dare not look upon the sky.
They are moles and owls: they call upon the soot
To cover them.

LUCIAN.   You cannot understand
The greatness of this people, Cetewayo.
You are a savage, reasoning like a child.
Each pallid English face conceals a brain
Whose powers are proven in the works of Newton
And in the plays of the immortal Shakespear.
There is not one of all the thousands here
But, if you placed him naked in the desert,
Would presently construct a steam engine,
And lay a cable t' th' Antipodes.

CETEWAYO. Have I been brought a million miles by sea
To learn how men can lie! Know, Father Webber,
Men become civilized through twin diseases,

Terror and Greed to wit: these two conjoined
Become the grisly parents of Invention.
Why does the trembling white with frantic toil
Of hand and brain produce the magic gun
That slays a mile off, whilst the manly Zulu
Dares look his foe i' the face; fights foot to foot;
Lives in the present; drains the Here and Now;
Makes life a long reality, and death
A moment only; whilst your Englishman
Glares on his burning candle's winding-sheets,
Counting the steps of his approaching doom,
And in the murky corners ever sees
Two horrid shadows, Death and Poverty:
In the which anguish an unnatural edge
Comes on his frighted brain, which straight devises
Strange frauds by which to filch unearnéd gold,
Mad crafts by which to slay unfacéd foes,
Until at last his agonized desire
Makes possibility its slave. And then—
Horrible climax! All-undoing spite!—
Th' importunate clutching of the coward's hand
From wearied Nature Devastation's secrets
Doth wrest; when straight the brave black-livered man
Is blown explosively from off the globe;
And Death and Dread, with their white-livered slaves,
Oer-run the earth, and through their chattering teeth
Stammer the words "Survival of the Fittest."
Enough of this: I came not here to talk.
Thou sayest thou hast two white-faced ones who dare
Fight without guns, and spearless, to the death.
Let them be brought.

  LUCIAN.   They fight not to the death,
But under strictest rules: as, for example,
Half of their persons shall not be attacked;
Nor shall they suffer blows when they fall down,
Nor stroke of foot at any time. And, further,

That frequent opportunities of rest
With succor and refreshment be secured them.

CETEWAYO. Ye gods, what cowards! Zululand, my Zululand:
Personified Pusillanimity
Hath taen thee from the bravest of the brave!

LUCIAN. Lo the rude savage whose untutored mind
Cannot perceive self-evidence, and doubts
That Brave and English mean the self-same thing!

CETEWAYO. Well, well, produce these heroes. I surmise
They will be carried by their nurses, lest
Some barking dog or bumbling bee should scare them.

CETEWAYO *takes his state. Enter* PARADISE

LYDIA. What hateful wretch is this whose mighty thews
Presage destruction to his adversaries.

LORD WORTHINGTON. Tis Paradise.

LYDIA.   He of whom Cashel spoke?
A dreadful thought ices my heart. Oh, why
Did Cashel leave us at the door?

Enter CASHEL

LORD WORTHINGTON.   Behold!
The champion comes.

LYDIA.   Oh, I could kiss him now
Here, before all the world. His boxing things
Render him most attractive. But I fear
Yon villain's fists may maul him.

WORTHINGTON.   Have no fear.
Hark! the king speaks.

CETEWAYO.   Ye sons of the white queen:
Tell me your names and deeds ere ye fall to.

PARADISE. Your royal highness, you beholds a bloke
What gets his living honest by his fists.
I may not have the polish of some toffs
As I could mention on; but up to now
No man has took my number down. I scale
Close on twelve stun; my age is twenty-three;

And at Bill Richardson's Blue Anchor pub
Am to be heard of any day by such
As likes the job. I dont know, governor,
As ennythink remains for me to say.

    CETEWAYO. Six wives and thirty oxen shalt thou have
If on the sand thou leave thy foeman dead.
Methinks he looks full scornfully on thee.
[*To Cashel*] Ha! dost thou not so?

    CASHEL.   Sir, I do beseech you
To name the bone, or limb, or special place
Where you would have me hit him with this fist.

    CETEWAYO. Thou hast a noble brow; but much I fear
Thine adversary will disfigure it.

    CASHEL. Theres a divinity that shapes our ends
Rough hew them how we will. Give me the gloves.

    THE MASTER OF THE REVELS. Paradise, a professor. Cashel Byron,
Also professor. Time!   [*They spar.*

    LYDIA.   Eternity
It seems to me until this fight be done.

    CASHEL. Dread monarch: this is called the upper cut,
And this is a hook-hit of mine own invention.
The hollow region where I plant this blow
Is called the mark. My left, you will observe,
I chiefly use for long shots: with my right
Aiming beside the angle of the jaw
And landing with a certain delicate screw
I without violence knock my foeman out.
Mark how he falls forward upon his face!
The rules allow ten seconds to get up;
And as the man is still quite silly, I
Might safely finish him; but my respect
For your most gracious majesty's desire
To see some further triumphs of the science
Of self-defence postpones awhile his doom.

    PARADISE. How can a bloke do hisself proper justice
With pillows on his fists?

[He tears off his gloves and attacks Cashel
with his bare knuckles.

THE CROWD. Unfair! The rules!

CETEWAYO. The joy of battle surges boiling up
And bids me join the mellay. Isandhlana
And Victory! *[He falls on the bystanders.*

THE CHIEFS. Victory and Isandhlana!

[They run amok. General panic and stampede.
The ring is swept away.

LUCIAN. Forbear these most irregular proceedings.
Police! Police!

[He engages Cetewayo with his umbrella. The balcony comes
down with a crash. Screams from its occupants. Indescribable
confusion.

CASHEL [*dragging Lydia from the struggling heap*] My love, my
love, art hurt?

LYDIA. No, no; but save my sore oermatchéd cousin.

A POLICEMAN. Give us a lead, sir. Save the English flag.
Africa tramples on it.

CASHEL. Africa!
Not all the continents whose mighty shoulders
The dancing diamonds of the seas bedeck
Shall trample on the blue with spots of white.
Now, Lydia, mark thy lover. *[He charges the Zulus.*

LYDIA. Hercules
Cannot withstand him. See: the king is down;
The tallest chief is up, heels over head,
Tossed corklike oer my Cashel's sinewy back;
And his lieutenant all deflated gasps
For breath upon the sand. The others fly.
In vain: his fist oer magic distances
Like a chameleon's tongue shoots to its mark;
And the last African upon his knees
Sues piteously for quarter. [*Rushing into Cashel's arms*]
Oh, my hero:
Thoust saved us all this day.

CASHEL. Twas all for thee.

CETEWAYO [*trying to rise*] Have I been struck by lightning?

LUCIAN. Sir, your conduct
Can only be described as most ungentlemanly.

POLICEMAN. One of the prone is white.

CASHEL. Tis Paradise.

POLICEMAN. He's choking: he has something in his mouth.

LYDIA [*to Cashel*] Oh Heaven! there is blood upon your hip.
Youre hurt.

CASHEL. The morsel in yon wretch's mouth
Was bitten out of me.

[*Sensation. Lydia screams and swoons in Cashel's arms.*

ACT III

Wiltstoken. A room in the Warren Lodge
Lydia at her writing-table

LYDIA. O Past and Present, how ye do conflict
As here I sit writing my father's life!
The autumn woodland woos me from without
With whispering of leaves and dainty airs
To leave this fruitless haunting of the past.
My father was a very learnéd man.
I sometimes think I shall oldmaided be
Ere I unlearn the things he taught to me.

Enter POLICEMAN

POLICEMAN. Asking your ladyship to pardon me
For this intrusion, might I be so bold
As ask a question of your people here
Concerning the Queen's peace?
LYDIA.   My people here
Are but a footman and a simple maid;
And both have craved a holiday to join
Some local festival. But, sir, your helmet
Proclaims the Metropolitan Police.
POLICEMAN. Madam, it does; and I may now inform you
That what you term a local festival
Is a most hideous outrage gainst the law,
Which we to quell from London have come down:
In short, a prizefight. My sole purpose here
Is to inquire whether your ladyship
Any bad characters this afternoon
Has noted in the neighborhood.
LYDIA.   No, none, sir.
I had not let my maid go forth today
Thought I the roads unsafe.
POLICEMAN.   Fear nothing, madam:

The force protects the fair. My mission here
Is to wreak ultion for the broken law.
I wish your ladyship good afternoon.

    LYDIA. Good afternoon.   [*Exit* POLICEMAN.
                    A prizefight! O my heart!
Cashel: hast thou deceived me? Can it be
Thou hast backslidden to the hateful calling
I asked thee to eschew?
                 O wretched maid,
Why didst thou flee from London to this place
To write thy father's life, whenas in town
Thou mightst have kept a guardian eye on him—
Whats that? A flying footstep—

Enter CASHEL

    CASHEL.   Sanctuary!
The law is on my track. What! Lydia here!

    LYDIA. Ay: Lydia here. Hast thou done murder, then,
That in so horrible a guise thou comest?

    CASHEL. Murder! I would I had. Yon cannibal
Hath forty thousand lives; and I have taen
But thousands thirty-nine. I tell thee, Lydia,
On the impenetrable sarcolobe
That holds his seedling brain these fists have pounded
By Shrewsb'ry clock an hour. This bruiséd grass
And cakéd mud adhering to my form
I have acquired in rolling on the sod
Clinched in his grip. This scanty reefer coat
For decency snatched up as fast I fled
When the police arrived, belongs to Mellish.
Tis all too short; hence my display of rib
And forearm mother-naked. Be not wroth
Because I seem to wink at you: by Heaven,
Twas Paradise that plugged me in the eye
Which I perforce keep closing. Pity me,
My training wasted and my blows unpaid.

119

Sans stakes, sans victory, sans everything
I had hoped to win. Oh, I could sit me down
And weep for bitterness.

LYDIA. Thou wretch, begone.

CASHEL. Begone!

LYDIA. I say begone. Oh, tiger's heart
Wrapped in a young man's hide, canst thou not live
In love with Nature and at peace with Man?
Must thou, although thy hands were never made
To blacken other's eyes, still batter at
The image of Divinity? I loathe thee.
Hence from my house and never see me more.

CASHEL. I go. The meanest lad on thy estate
Would not betray me thus. But tis no matter.

[He opens the door.
Ha! the police. I'm lost. *[He shuts the door again.*
Now shalt thou see
My last fight fought. Exhausted as I am,
To capture me will cost the coppers dear.
Come one, come all!

LYDIA. Oh, hide thee, I implore:
I cannot see thee hunted down like this.
There is my room. Conceal thyself therein.
Quick, I command. *[He goes into the room.*
With horror I foresee,
Lydia, that never lied, must lie for thee.

Enter POLICEMAN, *with* PARADISE *and* MELLISH *in custody,*
BASHVILLE, *constables, and others*

POLICEMAN. Keep back your bruiséd prisoner lest he shock
This wellbred lady's nerves. Your pardon, maam;
But have you seen by chance the other one?
In this direction he was seen to run.

LYDIA. A man came here anon with bloody hands
And aspect that did turn my soul to snow.

POLICEMAN. Twas he. What said he?

LYDIA. Begged for sanctuary.
I bade the man begone.

POLICEMAN. Most properly.
Saw you which way he went?

LYDIA. I cannot tell.

PARADISE. He seen me coming; and he done a bunk.

POLICEMAN. Peace, there. Excuse his damaged features, lady:
He's Paradise; and this one's Byron's trainer,
Mellish.

MELLISH. Injurious copper, in thy teeth
I hurl the lie. I am no trainer, I.
My father, a respected missionary,
Apprenticed me at fourteen years of age
T' the poetry writing. To these woods I came
With Nature to commune. My revery
Was by a sound of blows rudely dispelled.
Mindful of what my sainted parent taught
I rushed to play the peacemaker, when lo!
These minions of the law laid hands on me.

BASHVILLE. A lovely woman, with distracted cries,
In most resplendent fashionable frock,
Approaches like a wounded antelope.

Enter ADELAIDE GISBORNE

ADELAIDE. Where is my Cashel? Hath he been arrested?

POLICEMAN. I would I had thy Cashel by the collar:
He hath escaped me.

ADELAIDE. Praises be for ever!

LYDIA. Why dost thou call the missing man thy Cashel?

ADELAIDE. He is mine only son.

ALL. Thy son!

ADELAIDE. My son.

LYDIA. I thought his mother hardly would have known him,
So crushed his countenance.

ADELAIDE. A ribald peer,
Lord Worthington by name, this morning came

With honeyed words beseeching me to mount
His four-in-hand, and to the country hie
To see some English sport. Being by nature
Frank as a child, I fell into the snare,
But took so long to dress that the design
Failed of its full effect; for not until
The final round we reached the horrid scene.
Be silent all; for now I do approach
My tragedy's catastrophe. Know, then,
That Heaven did bless me with an only son,
A boy devoted to his doting mother—

POLICEMAN. Hark! did you hear an oath from yonder room?

ADELAIDE. Respect a broken-hearted mother's grief,
And do not interrupt me in my scene.
Ten years ago my darling disappeared
(Ten dreary twelvemonths of continuous tears,
Tears that have left me prematurely aged;
For I am younger far than I appear).
Judge of my anguish when today I saw
Stripped to the waist, and fighting like a demon
With one who, whatsoe'er his humble virtues,
Was clearly not a gentleman, my son!

ALL. O strange event! O passing tearful tale!

ADELAIDE. I thank you from the bottom of my heart
For the reception you have given my woe;
And now I ask, where is my wretched son?
He must at once come home with me, and quit
A course of life than cannot be allowed.

Enter CASHEL.

CASHEL. Policeman: I do yield me to the law.

LYDIA. Oh no.

ADELAIDE.   My son!

CASHEL.   My mother! Do not kiss me.
My visage is too sore.

POLICEMAN.   The lady hid him.

This is a regular plant. You cannot be
Up to that sex. [*To Cashel*] You come along with me.

LYDIA. Fear not, my Cashel: I will bail thee out.

CASHEL. Never. I do embrace my doom with joy.
With Paradise in Pentonville or Portland
I shall feel safe: there are no mothers there.

ADELAIDE. Ungracious boy—

CASHEL. Constable: bear me hence.

MELLISH. Oh, let me sweetest reconcilement make
By calling to thy mind that moving song:—
[*Sings*] They say there is no other—

CASHEL. Forbear at once, or the next note of music
That falls upon thine ear shall clang in thunder
From the last trumpet.

ADELAIDE. A disgraceful threat
To level at this virtuous old man.

LYDIA. Oh, Cashel, if thou scornst thy mother thus,
How wilt thou treat thy wife?

CASHEL. There spake my fate:
I knew you would say that. Oh, mothers, mothers,
Would you but let your wretched sons alone
Life were worth living! Had I any choice
In this importunate relationship?
None. And until that high auspicious day
When the millennium on an orphaned world
Shall dawn, and man upon his fellow look,
Reckless of consanguinity, my mother
And I within the self-same hemisphere
Conjointly may not dwell.

ADELAIDE. Ungentlemanly!

CASHEL. I am no gentleman. I am a criminal,
Redhanded, baseborn—

ADELAIDE. Baseborn! Who dares say it?
Thou art the son and heir of Bingley Bumpkin
FitzAlgernon de Courcy Cashel Byron,
Sieur of Park Lane and Overlord of Dorset,

Who after three months wedded happiness
Rashly fordid himself with prussic acid,
Leaving a tearstained note to testify
That having sweetly honeymooned with me,
He now could say, O Death, where is thy sting?
 POLICEMAN. Sir: had I known your quality, this cop
I had averted; but it is too late.
The law's above us both.

   Enter LUCIAN, *with an Order in Council*

 LUCIAN.   Not so, policeman.
I bear a message from The Throne itself
Of fullest amnesty for Byron's past.
Nay, more: of Dorset deputy lieutenant
He is proclaimed. Further, it is decreed,
In memory of his glorious victory
Over our country's foes at Islington,
The flag of England shall for ever bear
On azure field twelve swanlike spots of white;
And by an exercise of feudal right
Too long disused in this anarchic age
Our sovereign doth confer on him the hand
Of Miss Carew, Wiltstoken's wealthy heiress.
        [General acclamation.
 POLICEMAN. Was anything, sir, said about me?
 LUCIAN. Thy faithful services are not forgot:
In future call thyself Inspector Smith
        [Renewed acclamation.
 POLICEMAN. I thank you, sir. I thank you, gentlemen.
 LUCIAN. My former opposition, valiant champion,
Was based on the supposed discrepancy
Betwixt your rank and Lydia's. Heres my hand.
 BASHVILLE. And I do here unselfishly renounce
All my pretensions to my lady's favor. *[Sensation.*
 LYDIA. What, Bashville! didst thou love me?
 BASHVILLE.   Madam: yes.

Tis said: now let me leave immediately.

LYDIA. In taking, Bashville, this most tasteful course
You are but acting as a gentleman
In the like case would act. I fully grant
Your perfect right to make a declaration
Which flatters me and honors your ambition.
Prior attachment bids me firmly say
That whilst my Cashel lives, and polyandry
Rests foreign to the British social scheme,
Your love is hopeless; still, your services,
Made zealous by disinterested passion,
Would greatly add to my domestic comfort;
And if—

CASHEL. Excuse me. I have other views.
Ive noted in this man such aptitude
For art and exercise in his defence
That I prognosticate for him a future
More glorious than my past. Henceforth I dub him
The Admirable Bashville, Byron's Novice;
And to the utmost of my mended fortunes
Will back him gainst the world at ten stone six.

ALL. Hail, Byron's Novice, champion that shall be!

BASHVILLE. Must I renounce my lovely lady's service,
And mar the face of man?

CASHEL.   Tis Fate's decree.
For know, rash youth, that in this star crost world
Fate drives us all to find our chiefest good
In what we can, and not in what we would.

POLICEMAN. A post-horn—hark!

CASHEL.   What noise of wheels is this?

*Lord Worthington drives upon the scene in his
four-in-hand, and descends*

ADELAIDE. Perfidious peer!

LORD WORTHINGTON.   Sweet Adelaide—

ADELAIDE.   Forbear,

Audacious one: my name is Mrs Byron.

LORD WORTHINGTON. Oh, change that title for the sweeter one
Of Lady Worthington.

CASHEL.   Unhappy man,
You know not what you do.

LYDIA.   •   Nay, tis a match
Of must auspicious promise. Dear Lord Worthington,
You tear from us our mother-in-law—

CASHEL.   Ha! True.

LYDIA. —but we will make the sacrifice. She blushes:
At least she very prettily produces
Blushing's effect.

ADELAIDE.   My lord: I do accept you.

[*They embrace. Rejoicings.*

CASHEL [*aside*] It wrings my heart to see my noble backer
Lay waste his future thus. The world's a chessboard,
And we the merest pawns in fist of Fate.
[*Aloud*] And now, my friends, gentle and simple both,
Our scene draws to a close. In lawful course
As Dorset's deputy lieutenant I
Do pardon all concerned this afternoon
In the late gross and brutal exhibition
Of miscalled sport.

LYDIA [*throwing herself into his arms*] Your boats are burnt
at last.

CASHEL. This is the face that burnt a thousand boats,
And ravished Cashel Byron from the ring.
But to conclude. Let William Paradise
Devote himself to science, and acquire,
By studying the player's speech in Hamlet,
A more refined address. You, Robert Mellish,
To the Blue Anchor hostelry attend him;
Assuage his hurts, and bid Bill Richardson
Limit his access to the fatal tap.
Now mount we on my backer's four-in-hand,
And to St George's Church, whose portico

126

Hanover Square shuts off from Conduit Street,
Repair we all. Strike up the wedding march;
And, Mellish, let thy melodies trill forth
Broad oer the wold as fast we bowl along.
Give me the post-horn. Loose the flowing rein;
And up to London drive with might and main.

[Exeunt.

PRESS CUTTINGS

A TOPICAL SKETCH COMPILED FROM THE EDITORIAL
AND CORRESPONDENCE COLUMNS OF THE DAILY
PAPERS DURING THE WOMEN'S WAR IN 1909

By direction of the Lord Chamberlain the General and the Prime Minister in this play must in all public performances of it be addressed and described as General Bones and Mr Johnson, and by no means as General Mitchener and Mr Balsquith. The allusions to commoner persons are allowed to stand as they are.

General Mitchener, by the way, is not the late Lord Kitchener, but an earlier and more highly connected commander. Balsquith (Balfour-Asquith) is obviously neither of these statesmen, and cannot in the course of nature be both.

PRESS CUTTINGS

The forenoon of the first of April, three years hence.

General Mitchener is at his writing-table in the War Office, opening letters. On his left is the fireplace, with a fire burning. On his right, against the opposite wall, is a standing desk with an office stool. The door is in the wall behind him, half way between the table and the desk. The table is not quite in the middle of the room: it is nearer to the hearthrug than to the desk. There is a chair at each end of it for persons having business with the General. There is a telephone on the table.

Long silence.

A VOICE FROM THE STREET. Votes for Women!

The General starts convulsively; snatches a revolver from a drawer; and listens in an agony of apprehension. Nothing happens. He puts the revolver back, ashamed; wipes his brow; and resumes his work. He is startled afresh by the entry of an Orderly. This Orderly is an unsoldierly, slovenly, discontented young man.

MITCHENER. Oh, it's only you. Well?

THE ORDERLY. Another one, sir. She's chained herself.

MITCHENER. Chained herself? How? To what? Weve taken away the railings and everything that a chain can be passed through.

THE ORDERLY. We forgot the door-scraper, sir. She lay down on the flags and got the chain through before she started hollerin. She's lyin there now; and she downfaces us that youve got the key of the padlock in a letter in a buff envelope, and that youll see her when you open it.

MITCHENER. She's mad. Have the scraper dug up and let her go home with it hanging round her neck.

THE ORDERLY. There is a buff envelope there, sir.

MITCHENER. Youre all afraid of these women. [*He picks the letter up*] It does seem to have a key in it. [*He opens the letter; takes out a key and a note; and reads*] "Dear Mitch"—Well, I'm dashed!

131

THE ORDERLY. Yes, sir.

MITCHENER. What do you mean by Yes, sir?

THE ORDERLY. Well, you said you was dashed, sir; and you did look—if youll excuse my saying it, sir—well, you looked it.

MITCHENER [*who has been reading the letter, and is too astonished to attend to the Orderly's reply*] This is a letter from the Prime Minister asking me to release the woman with this key if she padlocks herself, and to have her shewn up and see her at once.

THE ORDERLY [*tremulously*] Dont do it, governor.

MITCHENER [*angrily*] How often have I ordered you not to address me as governor? Remember that you are a soldier and not a vulgar civilian. Remember also that when a man enters the army he leaves fear behind him. Heres the key. Unlock her and shew her up.

THE ORDERLY. Me unlock her! I dursent. Lord knows what she'd do to me.

MITCHENER [*pepperily, rising*] Obey your orders instantly, sir; and dont presume to argue. Even if she kills you, it is your duty to die for your country. Right about face. March.

The Orderly goes out, trembling.

THE VOICE OUTSIDE. Votes for Women! Votes for Women! Votes for Women!

MITCHENER [*mimicking her*] Votes for Women! Votes for Women! Votes for Women! [*In his natural voice*] Votes for children! Votes for babies! Votes for monkeys! [*He posts himself on the hearthrug and awaits the enemy*].

THE ORDERLY [*outside*] In you go. [*He pushes a panting Suffraget into the room*] The person, sir. [*He withdraws*].

The Suffraget takes off her tailor-made skirt and reveals a pair of fashionable trousers.

MITCHENER [*horrified*] Stop, madam. What are you doing? you must not undress in my presence. I protest. Not even your letter from the Prime Minister—

THE SUFFRAGET. My dear Mitchener: I am the Prime Minister. [*He takes off his hat and cloak; throws them on the desk; and confronts the General in the ordinary costume of a Cabinet Minister*].

MITCHENER. Good heavens! Balsquith!

BALSQUITH [*throwing himself into Mitchener's chair*] Yes: it is indeed Balsquith. It has come to this: that the only way the Prime Minister of England can get from Downing Street to the War Office is by assuming this disguise; shrieking "VOTES FOR WOMEN"; and chaining himself to your doorscraper. They were at the corner in force. They cheered me. Bellachristina herself was there. She shook my hand and told me to say I was a vegetarian, as the diet was better in Holloway for vegetarians.

MITCHENER. Why didnt you telephone?

BALSQUITH. They tap the telephone. Every switchboard in London is in their hands, or in those of their young men.

MITCHENER. Where on earth did you get the dress? I hope it's not a French dress!

BALSQUITH. Great heavens, no. We're not allowed even to put on our gloves with French chalk. Everything's labelled "Made in Camberwell."

MITCHENER. As a Tariff Reformer, I must say Quite right. [*Balsquith has a strong controversial impulse and is evidently going to dispute this profession of faith*]. No matter. Dont argue. What have you come for?

BALSQUITH. Sandstone has resigned.

MITCHENER [*amazed*] Old Red resigned!

BALSQUITH. Resigned.

MITCHENER. But how? Why? Oh, impossible! the proclamation of martial law last Tuesday made Sandstone virtually Dictator in the metropolis; and to resign now is flat desertion.

BALSQUITH. Yes, yes, my dear Mitchener: I know all that as well as you do: I argued with him until I was black in the face, and he so red about the neck that if I had gone on he would have burst. He is furious because we have abandoned his plan.

MITCHENER. But you accepted it unconditionally.

BALSQUITH. Yes, before we knew what it was. It was unworkable, you know.

MITCHENER. I dont know. Why is it unworkable?

BALSQUITH. I mean the part about drawing a cordon round

Westminster at a distance of two miles, and turning all women out of it.

MITCHENER. A masterpiece of strategy. Let me explain. The Suffragets are a very small body; but they are numerous enough to be troublesome—even dangerous—when they are all concentrated in one place—say in Parliament Square. But by making a two-mile radius and pushing them beyond it, you scatter their attack over a circular line twelve miles long. Just what Wellington would have done.

BALSQUITH. But the women wont go.

MITCHENER. Nonsense: they must go.

BALSQUITH. They wont.

MITCHENER. What does Sandstone say?

BALSQUITH. He says: Shoot them down.

MITCHENER. Of course.

BALSQUITH. Youre not serious?

MITCHENER. I'm perfectly serious.

BALSQUITH. But you cant shoot them down! Women, you know!

MITCHENER [*straddling confidently*] Yes you can. Strange as it may seem to you as a civilian, Balsquith, if you point a rifle at a woman and fire it, she will drop exactly as a man drops.

BALSQUITH. But suppose your own daughters—Helen and Georgina—

MITCHENER. My daughters would not dream of disobeying the proclamation. [*As an afterthought*] At least Helen wouldnt.

BALSQUITH. But Georgina?

MITCHENER. Georgina would if she knew she'd be shot if she didnt. Thats how the thing would work. Military methods are really the most merciful in the end. You keep sending these misguided women to Holloway and killing them slowly and inhumanly by ruining their health; and it does no good: they go on worse than ever. Shoot a few, promptly and humanely; and there will be an end at once of all resistance and of all the suffering that resistance entails.

BALSQUITH. But public opinion would never stand it.

MITCHENER [*walking about and laying down the law*] Theres no such thing as public opinion.

BALSQUITH. No such thing as public opinion!!

MITCHENER. Absolutely no such thing. There are certain persons who entertain certain opinions. Well, shoot them down. When you have shot them down, there are no longer any persons entertaining those opinions alive; consequently there is no longer any more of the public opinion you are so much afraid of. Grasp that fact, my dear Balsquith; and you have grasped the secret of government. Public opinion is mind. Mind is inseparable from matter. Shoot down the matter and you kill the mind.

BALSQUITH. But hang it all—

MITCHENER [*intolerantly*] No I wont hang it all. It's no use coming to me and talking about public opinion. You have put yourself into the hands of the army; and you are committed to military methods. And the basis of all military methods is that when people wont do what theyre told to do, you shoot them down.

BALSQUITH. Oh yes; it's all jolly fine for you and Old Red. You dont depend on votes for your places. What do you suppose would happen at the next election?

MITCHENER. Have no next election. Bring in a Bill at once repealing all the Reform Acts and vesting the Government in a properly trained magistracy responsible only to a Council of War. It answers perfectly in India. If anyone objects, shoot him down.

BALSQUITH. But none of the members of my party would be on the Council of War. Neither should I. Do you expect us to vote for making ourselves nobodies?

MITCHENER. Youll have to, sooner or later, or the Socialists will make nobodies of the lot of you by collaring every penny you possess. Do you suppose this damned democracy can be allowed to go on now that the mob is beginning to take it seriously and using its power to lay hands on property? Parliament must abolish itself. The Irish parliament voted for its own extinction. The English parliament will do the same if the same means are taken to persuade it.

BALSQUITH. That would cost a lot of money.

MITCHENER. Not money necessarily. Bribe them with titles.

BALSQUITH. Do you think we dare?

MITCHENER [*scornfully*] Dare! Dare! What is life but daring, man? "To dare, to dare, and again to dare—"

FEMALE VOICE IN THE STREET. Votes for Women! [*Mitchener, revolver in hand, rushes to the door and locks it. Balsquith hides under the table*]. Votes for Women!

A shot is heard.

BALSQUITH [*emerging in the greatest alarm*] Good heavens, you havent given orders to fire on them: have you?

MITCHENER. No: but it's a sentinel's duty to fire on anyone who persists in attempting to pass without giving the word.

BALSQUITH [*wiping his brow*] This military business is really awful.

MITCHENER. Be calm, Balsquith. These things must happen: they save bloodshed in the long run, believe me. Ive seen plenty of it; and I know.

BALSQUITH. I havnt; and I dont know. I wish those guns didnt make such a devil of a noise. We must adopt Maxim's Silencer for the army rifles if we're going to shoot women. I really couldnt stand hearing it. [*Someone outside tries to open the door and then knocks*]. Whats that?

MITCHENER. Who's there?

THE ORDERLY. It's only me, governor. It's all right.

MITCHENER [*unlocking the door and admitting the Orderly, who comes between them*] What was it?

THE ORDERLY. Suffraget, sir.

BALSQUITH. Did the sentry shoot her?

THE ORDERLY. No, sir: she shot the sentry.

BALSQUITH [*relieved*] Oh: is that all?

MITCHENER [*most indignantly*] All! A civilian shoots down one of His Majesty's soldiers on duty; and the Prime Minister of England asks, Is that all?!!! Have you no regard for the sanctity of human life?

BALSQUITH [*much relieved*] Well, getting shot is what a soldier is for. Besides, he doesnt vote.

MITCHENER. Neither do the Suffragets.

BALSQUITH. Their husbands do. [*To the Orderly*] Did she kill him?

THE ORDERLY. No, sir. He got a stinger on his trousers, sir; but it didnt penetrate. He lost his temper a bit and put down his gun and clouted her head for her. So she said he was no gentleman; and we let her go, thinking she'd had enough, sir.

MITCHENER [*groaning*] Clouted her head! These women are making the army as lawless as themselves. Clouted her head indeed! A purely civil procedure.

THE ORDERLY. Any orders, sir?

MITCHENER. No. Yes. No. Yes: send everybody who took part in this disgraceful scene to the guard-room. No. I'll address the men on the subject after lunch. Parade them for that purpose: full kit. Dont grin at me, sir. Right about face. March.

The Orderly obeys and goes out.

BALSQUITH [*taking Mitchener affectionately by the arm and walking him persuasively to and fro*] And now, Mitchener, will you come to the rescue of the Government and take the command that Old Red has thrown up?

MITCHENER. How can I? You know that the people are devoted heart and soul to Sandstone. He is only bringing you "on the knee," as we say in the army. Could any other living man have persuaded the British nation to accept universal compulsory military service as he did last year? Why, even the Church refused exemption. He is supreme—omnipotent.

BALSQUITH. He was, a year ago. But ever since your book of reminiscences went into two more editions than his, and the rush for it led to the wrecking of the Times Book Club, you have become to all intents and purposes his senior. He lost ground by saying that the wrecking was got up by the booksellers. It shewed jealousy; and the public felt it.

MITCHENER. But I cracked him up in my book—you see I could do no less after the handsome way he cracked me up in his

—and I cant go back on it now. [*Breaking loose from Balsquith*] No: it's no use, Balsquith: he can dictate his terms to you.

BALSQUITH. Not a bit of it. That affair of the curate—

MITCHENER [*impatiently*] Oh, damn that curate. Ive heard of nothing but that wretched mutineer for a fortnight past. He's not a curate: whilst he's serving in the army he's a private soldier and nothing else. I really havnt time to discuss him further. I'm busy. Good morning. [*He sits down at his table and takes up his letters*].

BALSQUITH [*near the door*] I'm sorry you take that tone, Mitchener. Since you do take it, let me tell you frankly that I think Lieutenant Chubbs-Jenkinson shewed a great want of consideration for the Government in giving an unreasonable and unpopular order, and bringing compulsory military service into disrepute.

MITCHENER. No order is unreasonable; and all orders are unpopular.

BALSQUITH. When the leader of the Labor Party appealed to me and to the House last year not to throw away all the liberties of Englishmen by accepting compulsory military service without full civil rights for the soldier—

MITCHENER. Rot.

BALSQUITH. —I said that no British officer would be capable of abusing the authority with which it was absolutely necessary to invest him.

MITCHENER. Quite right.

BALSQUITH. That carried the House;—

MITCHENER. Naturally.

BALSQUITH. —and the feeling was that the Labor Party were soulless cads.

MITCHENER. So they are.

BALSQUITH. And now comes this unmannerly young whelp Chubbs-Jenkinson, the only son of what they call a soda king, and orders a curate to lick his boots. And when the curate punches his head, you first sentence him to be shot; and then make a great show of clemency by commuting it to a flogging.

What did you expect the curate to do?

MITCHENER [*throwing down his pen and his letters and jumping up to confront Balsquith*] His duty was perfectly simple. He should have obeyed the order; and then laid his complaint against the officer in proper form. He would have received the fullest satisfaction.

BALSQUITH. What satisfaction?

MITCHENER. Chubbs-Jenkinson would have been reprimanded. In fact, he was reprimanded. Besides, the man was thoroughly insubordinate. You cant deny that the very first thing he did when they took him down after flogging him was to walk up to Chubbs-Jenkinson and break his jaw. That shewed there was no use flogging him; so now he will get two years' hard labor; and serve him right!

BALSQUITH. I bet you a guinea he wont get even a week. I bet you another that Chubbs-Jenkinson apologizes abjectly. You evidently havnt heard the news.

MITCHENER. What news?

BALSQUITH. It turns out that the curate is well connected. [*Mitchener staggers at the shock. He reels into his chair and buries his face in his hands over the blotter*]. He has three aunts in the peerage; Lady Richmond's one of them [*Mitchener punctuates these announcements with heartrending groans*]; and they all adore him. The invitations for six garden parties and fourteen dances have been cancelled for all the subalterns in Chubbs's regiment. [*Mitchener attempts to shoot himself*].

BALSQUITH [*seizing the pistol*] No: your country needs you, Mitchener.

MITCHENER [*putting down the pistol*] For my country's sake. [*Balsquith, reassured, sits down*]. But what an infernal young fool Chubbs-Jenkinson is, not to know the standing of his man better! Why didnt he know? It was his business to know. He ought to be flogged.

BALSQUITH. Probably he will be, by the other subalterns.

MITCHENER. I hope so. Anyhow, out he goes. Out of the army. He or I.

BALSQUITH. Steady, steady. His father has subscribed a million to the party funds. We owe him a peerage.

MITCHENER. I dont care.

BALSQUITH. I do. How do you think parties are kept up? Not by the subscriptions of the local associations, I hope. They dont pay for the gas at the meetings.

MITCHENER. Man: can you not be serious? Here are we, face to face with Lady Richmond's grave displeasure; and you talk to me about gas and subscriptions. Her own nephew!!!!!

BALSQUITH [*gloomily*] It's unfortunate. He was at Oxford with Bobby Bessborough.

MITCHENER. Worse and worse. What shall we do?

A VOICE IN THE STREET. Votes for Women! Votes for Women!

A terrific explosion shakes the building. They take no notice.

MITCHENER [*breaking down*] You dont know what this means to me, Balsquith. I love the army. I love my country.

BALSQUITH. It certainly is rather awkward.

The Orderly comes in.

MITCHENER [*angrily*] What is it? How dare you interrupt us like this?

THE ORDERLY. Didnt you hear the explosion, sir?

MITCHENER. Explosion. What explosion? No: I heard no explosion: I have something more serious to attend to than explosions. Great Heavens! Lady Richmond's nephew has been treated like any common laborer; and while England is reeling under the shock, a private walks in and asks me if I heard an explosion.

BALSQUITH. By the way, what was the explosion?

THE ORDERLY. Only a sort of bombshell, sir.

BALSQUITH. Bombshell!

THE ORDERLY. A pasteboard one, sir. Full of papers with Votes for Women in red letters. Fired into the yard from the roof of the Alliance Office.

MITCHENER. Pooh! Go away. GO away.

The Orderly, bewildered, goes out.

BALSQUITH. Mitchener: you can save the country yet. Put on

your full dress uniform and your medals and orders and so forth. Get a guard of honor—something showy—horse guards or something of that sort; and call on the old girl—

MITCHENER. The old girl?

BALSQUITH. Well, Lady Richmond. Apologize to her. Ask her leave to accept the command. Tell her that youve made the curate your adjutant or your aide-de-camp or whatever is the proper thing. By the way, what can you make him?

MITCHENER. I might make him my chaplain. I dont see why I shouldnt have a chaplain on my staff. He shewed a very proper spirit in punching that young cub's head. I should have done the same myself.

BALSQUITH. Then Ive your promise to take command if Lady Richmond consents?

MITCHENER. On condition that I have a free hand. No nonsense about public opinion or democracy.

BALSQUITH. As far as possible, I think I may say yes.

MITCHENER [*rising intolerantly and going to the hearthrug*] That wont do for me. Dont be weak-kneed, Balsquith. You know perfectly well that the real government of this country is and always must be the government of the masses by the classes. You know that democracy is damned nonsense, and that no class stands less of it than the working class. You know that we are already discussing the steps that will have to be taken if the country should ever be face to face with the possibility of a Labor majority in Parliament. You know that in that case we should disfranchise the mob, and if they made a fuss, shoot them down. You know that if we need public opinion to support us, we can get any quantity of it manufactured in our papers by poor devils of journalists who will sell their souls for five shillings. You know—

BALSQUITH. Stop. Stop, I say. I dont know. That is the difference between your job and mine, Mitchener. After twenty years in the army a man thinks he knows everything. After twenty months in the Cabinet he knows that he knows nothing.

MITCHENER. We learn from history—

BALSQUITH. We learn from history that men never learn anything from history. That's not my own: it's Hegel.

MITCHENER. Who's Hegel?

BALSQUITH. Dead. A German philosopher. [*He half rises, but recollects something and sits down again*]. Oh, confound it: that reminds me. The Germans have laid down four more Dreadnoughts.

MITCHENER. Then you must lay down twelve.

BALSQUITH. Oh yes: it's easy to say that; but think of what theyll cost.

MITCHENER. Think of what it would cost to be invaded by Germany and forced to pay an indemnity of five hundred millions.

BALSQUITH. But you said that if you got compulsory military service there would be an end of the danger of invasion.

MITCHENER. On the contrary, my dear fellow, it increases the danger tenfold, because it increases German jealousy of our military supremacy.

BALSQUITH. After all, why should the Germans invade us?

MITCHENER. Why shouldnt they? What else has their army to do? What else are they building a navy for?

BALSQUITH. Well, we never think of invading Germany.

MITCHENER. Yes, we do. I have thought of nothing else for the last ten years. Say what you will, Balsquith, the Germans have never recognized, and until they get a stern lesson they never will recognize, the plain fact that the interests of the British Empire are paramount, and that the command of the sea belongs by nature to England.

BALSQUITH. But if they wont recognize it, what can I do?

MITCHENER. Shoot them down.

BALSQUITH. I cant shoot them down.

MITCHENER. Yes you can. You dont realize it; but if you fire a rifle into a German he drops just as surely as a rabbit does.

BALSQUITH. But dash it all, man, a rabbit hasnt got a rifle and a German has. Suppose he shoots you down.

MITCHENER. Excuse me, Balsquith; but that consideration is what we call cowardice in the army. A soldier always assumes that he is going to shoot, not to be shot.

BALSQUITH [*jumping up and walking about sulkily*] Oh come! I like to hear you military people talking of cowardice. Why, you spend your lives in an ecstasy of terror of imaginary invasions. I dont believe you ever go to bed without looking under it for a burglar.

MITCHENER [*calmly*] A very sensible precaution, Balsquith. I always take it; and, in consequence, Ive never been burgled.

BALSQUITH. Neither have I. Anyhow, dont you taunt me with cowardice. [*He posts himself on the hearthrug beside Mitchener, on his left*]. I never look under my bed for a burglar. I'm not always looking under the nation's bed for an invader. And if it comes to fighting, I'm quite willing to fight without being three to one.

MITCHENER. These are the romantic ravings of a Jingo civilian, Balsquith. At least youll not deny that the absolute command of the sea is essential to our security.

BALSQUITH. The absolute command of the sea is essential to the security of the principality of Monaco. But Monaco isnt going to get it.

MITCHENER. And consequently Monaco enjoys no security. What a frightful thing! How do the inhabitants sleep with the possibility of invasion, of bombardment, continually present to their minds? Would you have our English slumbers broken in the same way? Are we also to live without security?

BALSQUITH [*dogmatically*] Yes. Theres no such thing as security in the world; and there never can be as long as men are mortal. England will be secure when England is dead, just as the streets of London will be safe when theres no longer a man in her streets to be run over or a vehicle to run over him. When you military chaps ask for security you are crying for the moon.

MITCHENER [*very seriously*] Let me tell you, Balsquith, that in these days of aeroplanes and Zeppelin airships the question of the moon is becoming one of the greatest importance. It will be reached at no very distant date. Can you, as an Englishman, tamely contemplate the possibility of having to live under a German moon? The British flag must be planted there at all hazards.

BALSQUITH. My dear Mitchener, the moon is outside practical politics. I'd swop it for a coaling-station tomorrow with Germany or any other Power sufficiently military in its way of thinking to attach any importance to it.

MITCHENER [*losing his temper*] You are the friend of every country but your own.

BALSQUITH. Say nobody's enemy but my own. It sounds nicer. You really neednt be so horribly afraid of the other countries. Theyre all in the same fix as we are. I'm much more interested in the death-rate in Lambeth than in the German fleet.

MITCHENER. You darent say that in Lambeth.

BALSQUITH. I'll say it the day after you publish your scheme for invading Germany and repealing all the Reform Acts.

The Orderly comes in.

MITCHENER. What do you want?

THE ORDERLY. I dont want anything, governor, thank you. The secretary and president of the Anti-Suffraget League says they had an appointment with the Prime Minister, and that theyve been sent on here from Downing Street.

BALSQUITH [*going to the table*] Quite right. I forgot them. [*To Mitchener*] Would you mind my seeing them here? I feel extraordinarily grateful to these women for standing by us and facing the Suffragets, especially as they are naturally the gentler and timider sort of women. [*The Orderly moans*]. Did you say anything?

THE ORDERLY. No, sir.

BALSQUITH. Did you catch their names?

THE ORDERLY. Yes, sir. The president is Lady Corinthia Fanshawe; and the secretary is Mrs Banger.

MITCHENER [*abruptly*] Mrs what?

THE ORDERLY. Mrs Banger.

BALSQUITH. Curious that quiet people always seem to have violent names.

THE ORDERLY. Not much quiet about her, sir.

MITCHENER [*outraged*] Attention! Speak when youre spoken

to. Hold your tongue when youre not. Right about face. March. [*The Orderly obeys*]. Thats the way to keep these chaps up to the mark. [*The Orderly returns*]. Back again! What do you mean by this mutiny?

THE ORDERLY. What am I to say to the ladies, sir?

BALSQUITH. You dont mind my seeing them somewhere, do you?

MITCHENER. Not at all. Bring them in to see me when youve done with them. I understand that Lady Corinthia is a very fascinating woman. Who is she, by the way?

BALSQUITH. Daughter of Lord Broadstairs, the automatic turbine man. Gave quarter of a million to the party funds. She's musical and romantic and all that—dont hunt: hates politics: stops in town all the year round: one never sees her except at the opera and at musical at-homes and so forth.

MITCHENER. What a life! [*To the Orderly*] Where are the ladies?

THE ORDERLY. In No. 17, sir.

MITCHENER. Shew Mr Balsquith there; and send Mrs Farrell here.

THE ORDERLY [*calling into the corridor*] Mrs Farrell! [*To Balsquith*] This way, sir. [*He goes out with Balsquith*].

Mrs Farrell, a lean, highly respectable Irish charwoman of about fifty, comes in.

MITCHENER. Mrs Farrell: Ive a very important visit to pay: I shall want my full dress uniform and all my medals and orders and my presentation sword. There was a time when the British Army contained men capable of discharging these duties for their commanding officer. Those days are over. The compulsorily enlisted soldier runs to a woman for everything. I'm therefore reluctantly obliged to trouble you.

MRS FARRELL. Your meddles n ordhers n the crooked sword widh the ivory handle n your full dress uniform is in the waxworks in the Chamber o Military Glory over in the place they used to call the Banquetin Hall. I told you youd be sorry for sendin them away; and you told me to mind me own business. Youre wiser now.

MITCHENER. I am. I had not at that time discovered that you were the only person in the whole military establishment of this capital who could be trusted to remember where anything was, or to understand an order and obey it.

MRS FARRELL. It's no good flattherin me. I'm too old.

MITCHENER. Not at all, Mrs Farrell. How is your daughter?

MRS FARRELL. Which daughter?

MITCHENER. The one who has made such a gratifying success in the Music Halls.

MRS FARRELL. Theres no Music Halls nowadays: theyre Variety Theatres. She's got an offer of marriage from a young jook.

MITCHENER. Is it possible? What did you do?

MRS FARRELL. I told his mother on him.

MITCHENER. Oh! What did she say?

MRS FARRELL. She was as pleased as Punch. Thank Heaven, she says, he's got somebody thatll be able to keep him when the supertax is put up to twenty shillings in the pound.

MITCHENER. But your daughter herself? What did she say?

MRS FARRELL. Accepted him, of course. What else would a young fool like her do? He inthrojooced her to the Poet Laureate, thinkin she'd inspire him.

MITCHENER. Did she?

MRS FARRELL. Faith, I dunna. All I know is she walked up to him as bold as brass n said, "Write me a sketch, dear." Afther all the throuble Ive took with that child's manners she's no more notion how to behave herself than a pig. Youll have to wear General Sandstone's uniform: it's the only one in the place, because he wont lend it to the shows.

MITCHENER. But Sandstone's clothes wont fit me.

MRS FARRELL [unmoved] Then youll have to fit them. Why shouldnt they fitchya as well as they fitted General Blake at the Mansion House?

MITCHENER. They didnt fit him. He looked a frightful guy.

MRS FARRELL. Well, you must do the best you can with them. You cant exhibit your clothes and wear them too.

MITCHENER. And the public thinks the lot of a commanding officer a happy one! Oh, if they could only see the seamy side of it. [*He returns to his table to resume work*].

MRS FARRELL. If they could only see the seamy side o General Sandstone's uniform, where his flask rubs agen the buckle of his braces, theyd tell him he ought to get a new one. Let alone the way he swears at me.

MITCHENER. When a man has risked his life on eight battle-fields, Mrs Farrell, he has given sufficient proof of his self-control to be excused a little strong language.

MRS FARRELL. Would you put up with bad language from me because Ive risked me life eight times in childbed?

MITCHENER. My dear Mrs Farrell, you surely would not compare a risk of that harmless domestic kind to the fearful risks of the battlefield.

MRS FARRELL. I wouldnt compare risks run to bear livin people into the world to risks run to blow dhem out of it. A mother's risk is jooty: a soldier's is nothin but divilmint.

MITCHENER [*nettled*] Let me tell you, Mrs Farrell, that if the men did not fight, the women would have to fight themselves. We spare you that at all events.

MRS FARRELL. You cant help yourselves. If three-quarters of you was killed we could replace you with the help of the other quarter. If three-quarters of us was killed how many people would there be in England in another generation? If it wasnt for that, the men'd put the fightin on us just as they put all the other dhrudgery. What would you do if we was all kilt? Would you go to bed and have twins?

MITCHENER. Really, Mrs Farrell, you must discuss these questions with a medical man. You make me blush, positively.

MRS FARRELL [*grumbling to herself*] A good job too. If I could have made Farrell blush I wouldnt have had to risk me life so often. You n your risks n your bravery n your self-conthrol indeed. "Why dont you conthrol yourself?" I sez to Farrell. "It's agen me religion," he sez.

MITCHENER [*plaintively*] Mrs Farrell: youre a woman of very powerful mind. I'm not qualified to argue these delicate matters with you. I ask you to spare me, and to be good enough to take these clothes to Mr Balsquith when the ladies leave.

The Orderly comes in.

THE ORDERLY. Lady Corinthia Fanshawe and Mrs Banger want to see you, sir. Mr Balsquith told me to tell you.

MRS FARRELL. Theyve come about the vote. I dont know whether it's dhem dhat want it or dhem dhat doesnt want it: anyhow, theyre all alike when they get into a state about it. [*She goes out, having gathered Balsquith's Suffraget disguise from the desk*].

MITCHENER. Is Mr Balsquith not with them.

THE ORDERLY. No, sir. Couldnt stand Mrs Banger, I expect. Fair caution she is. [*Chuckling*] Couldnt help larfin when I sor im op it.

MITCHENER [*highly incensed*] How dare you indulge in this unseemly mirth in the presence of your commanding officer? Have you no sense of a soldier's duty?

THE ORDERLY [*sadly*] I'm afraid I shant ever get the ang of it, sir. You see, my father has a tidy little barber's business down off Shoreditch; and I was brought up to be chatty and easy-like with everybody. I tell you, when I drew the number in the conscription it gev my old mother the needle and it gev me the ump. I should take it very kind, sir, if youd let me off the drill and let me shave you instead. Youd appreciate my qualities then: you would indeed, sir. I shant never do myself jastice at soljerin, sir. I cant bring myself to think of it as proper work for a man with an active mind, as you might say, sir. Arf of it's only ousemaidin; and tother arf is dress-up and make-believe.

MITCHENER. Stuff, sir. It's the easiest life in the world. Once you learn your drill, all you have to do is to hold your tongue and obey your orders.

THE ORDERLY. But I do assure you, sir, arf the time theyre the wrong orders; and I get into trouble when I obey them. The sergeant's orders is all right; but the officers dont know what theyre talkin about. Why, the orses knows better sometimes. "Fours," says Lieutenant Trevor at the gate of Bucknam Palace only this mornin when we was on dooty for a State visit to the Coal Trust. I was fourth man like in the first file; and when I started the orse eld back; and the sergeant was on to me straight. Threes, you bally fool, e whispers. An e was on to me again about it when we come back, and called me a fathead, e did. What am I to do, I says: the lieutenant's orders was fours, I says. I'll shew you who's lieutenant here, e says. In future you attend to my orders and not to iz, e says: what does e know about it? e says. You didnt give me any orders, I says. Couldnt you see for yourself there wasnt room for fours, e says: why cant you think? General Mitchener tells me I'm not to think, but to obey orders, I says. Is Mitchener your sergeant or am I? e says in his bullyin way. You are, I says. Well, e says, you got to do what your sergeant tells you: thats discipline, e says. And what am I to do for the General? I says. Youre to let him talk, e says: thats what e's for.

MITCHENER [*groaning*] It is impossible for the human mind to conceive anything more dreadful than this. Youre a disgrace to the service.

THE ORDERLY [*deeply wounded*] The service is a disgrace to me. When my mother's people pass me in the street with this uniform on, I ardly know which way to look. There never was a soldier in my family before.

MITCHENER. There never was anything else in mine, sir.

THE ORDERLY. My mother's second cousin was one of the Parkinsons o Stepney. [*Almost in tears*] What do you know of the feelings of a respectable family in the middle station of life? I cant bear to be looked down on as a common soldier. Why cant my father be let buy my discharge? Youve done away with the soldier's right to ave his discharge bought for him by his relations. The country didnt know you were going to do that or it'd never ave stood it. Is an Englishman to be made a mockery like this?

MITCHENER. Silence. Attention. Right about face. March.

THE ORDERLY [*retiring to the standing desk and bedewing it with passionate tears*] Oh that I should have lived to be spoke to as

149

if I was the lowest of the low! Me! that has shaved a City o London alderman wiv me own and.

MITCHENER. Poltroon. Crybaby. Well, better disgrace yourself here than disgrace your country on the field of battle.

THE ORDERLY [*angrily coming to the table*] Who's going to disgrace his country on the field of battle? It's not fightin I object to: it's soljerin. Shew me a German and I'll ave a go at him as fast as you or any man. But to ave me time wasted like this, an be stuck in a sentry-box at a street corner for an ornament to be stared at; and to be told "right about face: march," if I speak as one man to another: that aint pluck: that aint fightin: that aint patriotism: it's bein made a bloomin sheep of.

MITCHENER. A sheep has many valuable military qualities. Emulate them, dont disparage them.

THE ORDERLY. Oh, wots the good of talkin to you? If I wasnt a poor soldier I could punch your ed for forty shillins or a month. But because youre my commandin officer you deprive me of my right to a magistrate, and make a compliment of giving me two years ard stead o shootin me. Why cant you take your chance the same as any civilian does?

MITCHENER [*rising majestically*] I search the pages of history in vain for a parallel to such a speech made by a private to a General. But for the coherence of your remarks I should conclude that you were drunk. As it is, you must be mad. You shall be placed under restraint at once. Call the guard.

THE ORDERLY. Call your grandmother. If you take one man off the doors the place'll be full of Suffragets before you can wink.

MITCHENER. Then arrest yourself; and off with you to the guard-room.

THE ORDERLY. What am I to arrest myself for?

MITCHENER. Thats nothing to you. You have your orders: obey them. Do you hear? Right about face. March.

THE ORDERLY. How would you feel if you was told to right-about-face and march as if you was a door-mat?

MITCHENER. I should feel as if my country had spoken through the voice of my officer. I should feel proud and honored to be able to serve my country by obeying its commands. No thought of self, no vulgar preoccupation with my own petty vanity, could touch my mind at such a moment. To me my officer would not be a mere man: he would be for the moment—whatever his personal frailties—the incarnation of our national destiny.

THE ORDERLY. What I'm saying to you is the voice of old England a jolly sight more than all this rot that you get out of books. I'd rather be spoke to by a sergeant than by you. He tells me to go to hell when I challenges him to argue it out like a man. It aint polite; but it's English. What you say aint anything at all. You dont act on it yourself. You dont believe in it. Youd punch my head if I tried it on you; and serve me right. And look here. Heres another point for you to argue—

MITCHENER [*with a shriek of protest*] No—

Mrs Banger comes in followed by Lady Corinthia Fanshawe. Mrs Banger is a masculine woman of forty with a powerful voice and great physical strength. Lady Corinthia, who is also over thirty, is beautiful and romantic.

MRS BANGER [*throwing the door open decisively and marching straight to Mitchener*] Pray how much longer is the Anti-Suffraget League to be kept waiting? [*She passes him contemptuously and sits down with impressive confidence in the chair next the fireplace. Lady Corinthia takes the chair on the opposite side of the table with equal aplomb*].

MITCHENER. I'm extremely sorry. You really do not know what I have to put up with. This imbecile, incompetent, un-soldierly disgrace to the uniform he should never have been allowed to put on, ought to have shewn you in fifteen minutes ago.

THE ORDERLY. All I said was—

MITCHENER. Not another word. Attention. Right about face. March. [*The Orderly sits down doggedly*]. Get out of the room this instant, you fool; or I'll kick you out.

THE ORDERLY [*civilly*] I dont mind that, sir. It's human. It's English. Why couldn't you have said it before? [*He goes out*].

MITCHENER. Take no notice, I beg: these scenes are of daily occurrence now that we have compulsory service under the command of the halfpenny papers. Pray sit down.

LADY CORINTHIA
AND MRS BANGER } [*rising*] { Thank you. [*They sit down again*].

MITCHENER [*sitting down with a slight chuckle of satisfaction*] And now, ladies, to what am I indebted—

MRS BANGER. Let me introduce us. I am Rosa Carmina Banger: Mrs Banger, organizing secretary of the Anti-Suffraget League. This is Lady Corinthia Fanshawe, the president of the League, known in musical circles—*I* am not musical—as the Richmond Park nightingale. A soprano. I am myself said to be almost a baritone; but I do not profess to understand these distinctions.

MITCHENER [*murmuring politely*] Most happy, I'm sure.

MRS BANGER. We have come to tell you plainly that the Anti-Suffragets are going to fight.

MITCHENER [*gallantly*] Oh, pray leave that to the men, Mrs Banger.

LADY CORINTHIA. We can no longer trust the men.

MRS BANGER. They have shewn neither the strength, the courage, nor the determination which are needed to combat women like the Suffragets.

LADY CORINTHIA. Nature is too strong for the combatants.

MRS BANGER. Physical struggles between persons of opposite sexes are unseemly.

LADY CORINTHIA. Demoralizing.

MRS BANGER. Insincere.

LADY CORINTHIA. They are merely embraces in disguise.

MRS BANGER. No such suspicion can attach to combats in which the antagonists are of the same sex.

LADY CORINTHIA. The Anti-Suffragets have resolved to take the field.

MRS BANGER. They will enforce the order of General Sandstone for the removal of all women from the two-mile radius—that is, all women except themselves.

MITCHENER. I am sorry to have to inform you, madam, that

the Government has given up that project, and that General Sandstone has resigned in consequence.

MRS BANGER. That does not concern us in the least. We approve of the project and will see that it is carried out. We have spent a good deal of money arming ourselves; and we are not going to have that money thrown away through the pusillanimity of a Cabinet of males.

MITCHENER. Arming yourselves! But, my dear ladies, under the latest proclamation women are strictly forbidden to carry chains, padlocks, tracts on the franchise, or weapons of any description.

LADY CORINTHIA [*producing an ivory-handled revolver and pointing it at his nose*] You little know your countrywomen, General Mitchener.

MITCHENER [*without flinching*] Madam: it is my duty to take possession of that weapon in accordance with the proclamation. Be good enough to put it down.

MRS BANGER [*producing an XVIII century horse pistol*] Is it your duty to take possession of this also?

MITCHENER. That, madam, is not a weapon: it is a curiosity. If you would be kind enough to place it in some museum instead of pointing it at my head, I should be obliged to you.

MRS BANGER. This pistol, sir, was carried at Waterloo by my grandmother.

MITCHENER. I presume you mean your grandfather.

MRS BANGER. You presume unwarrantably.

LADY CORINTHIA. Mrs Banger's grandmother commanded a canteen at that celebrated battle.

MRS BANGER. Who my grandfather was is a point that has never been quite clearly settled. I put my trust, not in my ancestors, but in my good sword, which is at my lodgings.

MITCHENER. Your sword!

MRS BANGER. The sword with which I slew five Egyptians with my own hand at Kassassin, where I served as a trooper.

MITCHENER. Lord bless me! But was your sex never discovered?

MRS BANGER. It was never even suspected. I had a comrade—

a gentleman ranker—whom they called Fanny. They never called me Fanny.

LADY CORINTHIA. The Suffragets have turned the whole woman movement on to the wrong track. They ask for a vote.

MRS BANGER. What use is a vote? Men have the vote.

LADY CORINTHIA. And men are slaves.

MRS BANGER. What women need is the right to military service. Give me a well-mounted regiment of women with sabres, opposed to a regiment of men with votes. We shall see which will go down before the other. No: we have had enough of these gentle pretty creatures who merely talk and cross-examine ministers in police courts, and go to prison like sheep, and suffer and sacrifice themselves. This question must be solved by blood and iron, as was well said by Bismarck, whom I have reason to believe was a woman in disguise.

MITCHENER. Bismarck a woman!

MRS BANGER. All the really strong men of history have been disguised women.

MITCHENER. [remonstrating] My dear lady!

MRS BANGER. How can you tell? You never knew that the hero of the charge at Kassassin was a woman: yet she was: it was I, Rosa Carmina Banger. Would Napoleon have been so brutal to women, think you, had he been a man?

MITCHENER. Oh, come, come! Really! Surely female rulers have often shewn all the feminine weaknesses. Queen Elizabeth, for instance. Her vanity, her levity—

MRS BANGER. Nobody who has studied the history of Queen Elizabeth can doubt for a moment that she was a disguised man.

LADY CORINTHIA [admiring Mrs Banger] Isnt she splendid!

MRS BANGER [rising with a large gesture] This very afternoon I shall cast off this hampering skirt for ever; mount my charger; and with my good sabre lead the Anti-Suffragets to victory. [She strides to the other side of the room, snorting].

MITCHENER. But I cant allow anything of the sort, madam. I shall stand no such ridiculous nonsense. I'm perfectly determined to put my foot down—

LADY CORINTHIA. Dont be hysterical, General.

MITCHENER. Hysterical!

MRS BANGER. Do you think we are to be stopped by these childish exhibitions of temper? They are useless; and your tears and entreaties—a man's last resource—will avail you just as little. I sweep them away, just as I sweep your plans of campaign "made in Germany"—

MITCHENER [*flying into a transport of rage*] How dare you repeat that infamous slander! [*He rings the bell violently*]. If this is the alternative to votes for women, I shall advocate giving every woman in the country six votes. [*The Orderly comes in*]. Remove that woman. See that she leaves the building at once.

The Orderly forlornly contemplates the iron front presented by Mrs Banger.

THE ORDERLY [*propitiatorily*] Would you ave the feelin art to step out, madam?

MRS BANGER. You are a soldier. Obey your orders. Put me out. If I got such an order I should not hesitate.

THE ORDERLY [*to Mitchener*] Would you mind lendin me a and, Guvner?

LADY CORINTHIA [*raising her revolver*] I shall be obliged to shoot you if you stir, General.

MRS BANGER [*to the Orderly*] When you are ordered to put a person out you should do it like this. [*She hurls him from the room. He is heard falling headlong downstairs and crashing through a glass door*]. I shall now wait on General Sandstone. If he shews any sign of weakness, he shall share that poor wretch's fate. [*She goes out*].

LADY CORINTHIA. Isnt she magnificent?

MITCHENER. Thank heaven she's gone. And now, my dear lady, is it necessary to keep that loaded pistol to my nose all through our conversation?

LADY CORINTHIA. It's not loaded. It's heavy enough, goodness knows, without putting bullets in it.

MITCHENER [*triumphantly snatching his revolver from the drawer*] Then I am master of the situation. This is loaded. Ha, ha!

LADY CORINTHIA. But since we are not really going to shoot one another, what difference can it possibly make?

MITCHENER [*putting his pistol down on the table*] True. Quite true. I recognize there the practical good sense that has prevented you from falling into the snares of the Suffragets.

LADY CORINTHIA. The Suffragets, General, are the dupes of dowdies. A really attractive and clever woman—

MITCHENER [*gallantly*] Yourself, for instance.

LADY CORINTHIA [*snatching up his revolver*] Another step and you are a dead man.

MITCHENER [*amazed*] My dear lady!

LADY CORINTHIA. I am not your dear lady. You are not the first man who has concluded that because I am devoted to music and can reach F in alt with the greatest facility—Patti never got above E flat—I am marked out as the prey of every libertine. You think I am like the thousands of weak women whom you have ruined—

MITCHENER. I solemnly protest—

LADY CORINTHIA. Oh, I know what you officers are. To you a woman's honor is nothing, and the idle pleasure of the moment is everything.

MITCHENER. This is perfectly ridiculous. I never ruined anyone in my life.

LADY CORINTHIA. Never! Are you in earnest?

MITCHENER. Certainly I am in earnest. Most indignantly in earnest.

LADY CORINTHIA [*throwing down the pistol contemptuously*] Then you have no temperament: you are not an artist. You have no soul for music.

MITCHENER. Ive subscribed to the regimental band all my life. I bought two sarrusophones for it out of my own pocket. When I sang Tosti's Goodbye for Ever at Knightsbridge in 1880 the whole regiment wept. You are too young to remember that.

LADY CORINTHIA. Your advances are useless. I—

MITCHENER. Confound it, madam, can you not receive an innocent compliment without suspecting me of dishonorable intentions?

LADY CORINTHIA. Love—real love—makes all intentions honorable. But you could never understand that.

MITCHENER. I'll not submit to the vulgar penny-novelette notion that an officer is less honorable than a civilian in his relations with women. While I live I'll raise my voice—

LADY CORINTHIA. Tush!

MITCHENER. What do you mean by tush?

LADY CORINTHIA. You cant raise your voice above its natural compass. What sort of voice have you?

MITCHENER. A tenor. What sort had you?

LADY CORINTHIA. Had! I have it still. I tell you I am the highest living soprano. [*Scornfully*] What was your highest note, pray?

MITCHENER. B flat—once—in 1879. I was drunk at the time.

LADY CORINTHIA [*gazing at him almost tenderly*] Though you may not believe me, I find you are more interesting when you talk about music than when you are endeavoring to betray a woman who has trusted you by remaining alone with you in your apartment.

MITCHENER [*springing up and fuming away to the fireplace*] Those repeated insults to a man of blameless life are as disgraceful to you as they are undeserved by me, Lady Corinthia. Such suspicions invite the conduct they impute. [*She raises the pistol*]. You need not be alarmed: I am only going to leave the room.

LADY CORINTHIA. Fish.

MITCHENER. Fish! This is worse than tush. Why fish?

LADY CORINTHIA. Yes, fish: cold-blooded fish.

MITCHENER. Dash it all, madam, do you want me to make advances to you?

LADY CORINTHIA. I have not the slightest intention of yielding to them; but to make them would be a tribute to romance. What is life without romance?

MITCHENER [*making a movement towards her*] I tell you—

LADY CORINTHIA. Stop. No nearer. No vulgar sensuousness. If you must adore, adore at a distance.

MITCHENER. This is worse than Mrs Banger. I shall ask that

estimable woman to come back.

LADY CORINTHIA. Poor Mrs Banger! Do not for a moment suppose, General Mitchener, that Mrs Banger represents my views on the suffrage question. Mrs Banger is a man in petticoats. I am every inch a woman; but I find it convenient to work with her.

MITCHENER. Do you find the combination comfortable?

LADY CORINTHIA. I do not wear combinations, General: [*with dignity*] they are unwomanly.

MITCHENER [*throwing himself despairingly into the chair next the hearthrug*] I shall go mad. I never for a moment dreamt of alluding to anything of the sort.

LADY CORINTHIA. There is no need to blush and become self-conscious at the mention of underclothing. You are extremely vulgar, General.

MITCHENER. Lady Corinthia: you have my pistol. Will you have the goodness to blow my brains out? I should prefer it to any other effort to follow the gyrations of the weathercock you no doubt call your mind. If you refuse, then I warn you that youll not get another word out of me—not if we sit here until doomsday.

LADY CORINTHIA. I dont want you to talk. I want you to listen. You do not understand my views on the question of the suffrage. [*She rises to make a speech*]. I must preface my remarks by reminding you that the Suffraget movement is essentially a dowdy movement. The Suffragets are not all dowdies; but they are mainly supported by dowdies. Now I am not a dowdy. Oh, no compliments—

MITCHENER. I did not utter a sound.

LADY CORINTHIA [*smiling*] It is easy to read your thoughts. I am one of those women who are accustomed to rule the world through men. Man is ruled by beauty, by charm. The men who are not have no influence. The Salic Law, which forbade women to occupy a throne, is founded on the fact that when a woman is on the throne the country is ruled by men, and therefore ruled badly; whereas when a man is on the throne the country is ruled by women, and therefore ruled well. The Suffragets would degrade women from being rulers to being voters, mere politicians, the drudges of the caucus and the polling booth. We should lose our influence completely under such a state of affairs. The New Zealand women have the vote. What is the result? No poet ever makes a New Zealand woman his heroine. One might as well be romantic about New Zealand mutton. Look at the Suffragets themselves. The only ones who are popular are the pretty ones, who flirt with mobs as ordinary women flirt with officers.

MITCHENER. Then I understand you to hold that the country should be governed by the women after all.

LADY CORINTHIA. Not by all the women. By certain women. I had almost said by one woman. By the women who have charm —who have artistic talent—who wield a legitimate, a refining influence over the men. [*She sits down gracefully, smiling, and arranging her draperies with conscious elegance*].

MITCHENER. In short, madam, you think that if you give the vote to the man, you give the power to the woman who can get round the man.

LADY CORINTHIA. That is not a very delicate way of putting it; but I suppose that is how you would express what I mean.

MITCHENER. Perhaps youve never had any experience of garrison life. If you had, youd have noticed that the sort of woman who's clever at getting round men is sometimes rather a bad lot.

LADY CORINTHIA. What do you mean by a bad lot?

MITCHENER. I mean a woman who would play the very devil if the other women didnt keep her in pretty strict order. I dont approve of democracy, because it's rot; and I'm against giving the vote to women, because I'm not accustomed to it, and therefore am able to see with an unprejudiced eye what infernal nonsense it is. But I tell you plainly, Lady Corinthia, that there is one game that I dislike more than either democracy or votes for women; and that is the game of Antony and Cleopatra. If I must be ruled by women, let me have decent women, and not— —well, not the other sort.

LADY CORINTHIA. You have a coarse mind, General Mitchener.

MITCHENER. So has Mrs Banger. And, by George! I prefer Mrs Banger to you!

LADY CORINTHIA [*bounding to her feet*] You prefer Mrs Banger to me!!!

MITCHENER. I do. You said yourself she was splendid.

LADY CORINTHIA. You are no true man. You are one of those unsexed creatures who have no joy in life, no sense of beauty, no high notes.

MITCHENER. No doubt I am, madam. As a matter of fact, I am not clever at discussing public questions, because, as an English gentleman, I was not brought up to use my brains. But occasionally, after a number of remarks which are perhaps sometimes rather idiotic, I get certain convictions. Thanks to you, I have now got a conviction that this woman question is not a question of lovely and accomplished females, but of dowdies. The average Englishwoman is a dowdy and never has half a chance of becoming anything else. She hasnt any charm; and she has no high notes, except when she's giving her husband a piece of her mind, or calling down the street for one of the children.

LADY CORINTHIA. How disgusting!

MITCHENER. Somebody must do the dowdy work! If we had to choose between pitching all the dowdies into the Thames and pitching all the lovely and accomplished women, the lovely ones would have to go.

LADY CORINTHIA. And if you had to do without Wagner's music or do without your breakfast, you would do without Wagner. Pray does that make eggs and bacon more precious than music, or the butcher and baker better than the poet and philosopher? The scullery may be more necessary to our bare existence than the cathedral. Even humbler apartments might make the same claim. But which is the more essential to the higher life?

MITCHENER. Your arguments are so devilishly ingenious that I feel convinced you got them out of some confounded book. Mine—such as they are—are my own. I imagine it's something like this. There is an old saying that if you take care of the pence, the pounds will take care of themselves. Well, perhaps if we take care of the dowdies and the butchers and the bakers, the beauties and the bigwigs will take care of themselves. [*Rising and facing her determinedly*] Anyhow, I dont want to have things arranged for me by Wagner. I'm not Wagner. How does he know where the shoe pinches me? How do you know where the shoe pinches your washerwoman? you and your high F in alt! How are you to know when you havnt made her comfortable unless she has a vote? Do you want her to come and break your windows?

LADY CORINTHIA. Am I to understand that General Mitchener is a Democrat and a Suffraget?

MITCHENER. Yes: you have converted me—you and Mrs Banger.

LADY CORINTHIA. Farewell, creature. [*Balsquith enters hurriedly*]. Mr Balsquith: I am going to wait on General Sandstone. He, at least, is an officer and a gentleman. [*She sails out*].

BALSQUITH. Mitchener: the game is up.

MITCHENER. What do you mean?

BALSQUITH. The strain is too much for the Cabinet. The old Liberal and Unionist Free Traders declare that if they are defeated on their resolution to invite tenders from private contractors for carrying on the Army and Navy, they will go solid for votes for women as the only means of restoring the liberties of the country which we have destroyed by compulsory military service.

MITCHENER. Infernal impudence!

BALSQUITH. The Labor Party is taking the same line. They say the men got the Factory Acts by hiding behind the women's petticoats, and that they will get votes for the army in the same way.

MITCHENER. Balsquith: we must not yield to clamor. I have just told that woman that I am at last convinced—

BALSQUITH [*joyfully*] —that the Suffragets must be supported?

MITCHENER. No: that the Anti-Suffragets must be put down at all hazards.

BALSQUITH. Same thing.

MITCHENER. No. For you now tell me that the Labor Party demands votes for women. That makes it impossible to give them, because it would be yielding to clamor. The one condition on which we can consent to grant anything in this country is that nobody shall presume to ask for it.

BALSQUITH [*earnestly*] Mitchener: it's no use. You cant have the conveniences of Democracy without its occasional inconveniences.

MITCHENER. What are its conveniences, I should like to know?

BALSQUITH. Well, when you tell people that they are the real rulers and they can do what they like, nine times out of ten they say "All right: tell us what to do." But it happens sometimes that they get an idea of their own; and then of course youre landed.

MITCHENER. Sh—

BALSQUITH [*desperately shouting him down*] No: it's no use telling me to shoot them down: I'm not going to do it. After all, I dont suppose votes for women will make much difference. It hasnt in the other countries in which it has been tried.

MITCHENER. I never supposed it would make any difference. What I cant stand is giving in to that Pankhurst lot. Hang it all, Balsquith, it seems only yesterday that we put them in quad for a month. I said at the time that it ought to have been ten years. If my advice had been taken this wouldnt have happened. It's a consolation to me that events are proving how thoroughly right I was.

The Orderly rushes in.

THE ORDERLY. Look 'ere, sir: Mrs Banger's locked the door of General Sandstone's room on the inside; an' she's sittin on his ed til he signs a proclamation for women to serve in the army.

MITCHENER. Put your shoulder to the door and burst it open.

THE ORDERLY. It's only in story books that doors burst open as easy as that. Besides, I'm only too thankful to av a locked door between me and Mrs B.; and so is all the rest of us.

MITCHENER. Cowards. Balsquith: to the rescue! [*He dashes out*].

BALSQUITH [*ambling calmly to the hearth*] This is the business of the Sergeant-at-Arms rather than of the leader of the House. Theres no use in my tackling Mrs Banger: she would only sit on my head too.

THE ORDERLY. You take my tip, Mr Balsquith. Give the women the vote and give the army civil rights; and av done with it.

Mitchener returns and comes between them.

MITCHENER. Balsquith: prepare to hear the worst.

BALSQUITH. Sandstone is no more?

MITCHENER. On the contrary, he is particularly lively. He has softened Mrs Banger by a proposal of marriage in which he appears to be perfectly in earnest. He says he has met his ideal at last, a really soldierly woman. She will sit on his head for the rest of his life; and the British Army is now to all intents and purposes commanded by Mrs Banger. When I remonstrated with Sandstone she positively shouted "Right about face. March" at me in the most offensive tone. If she hadnt been a woman I should have punched her head. I precious nearly punched Sandstone's. The horrors of martial law administered by Mrs Banger are too terrible to be faced. I demand civil rights for the army.

THE ORDERLY [*chuckling*] Wot oh, General! Wot oh!

MITCHENER. Hold your tongue. [*He goes to the door and calls*] Mrs Farrell! [*He returns, and again addresses the Orderly*]. Civil rights dont mean the right to be uncivil. [*Pleased with his own wit*] Almost a pun. Ha ha!

MRS FARRELL [*entering*] Whats the matther now? [*She comes to the table*].

MITCHENER [*to the Orderly*] I have private business with Mrs Farrell. Outside, you infernal blackguard.

THE ORDERLY [*arguing, as usual*] Well, I didnt ask to— [*Mitchener seizes him by the nape; marches him out; slams the door; and comes solemnly to Mrs Farrell*].

MITCHENER. Excuse the abruptness of this communication, Mrs Farrell; but I know only one woman in the country whose practical ability and force of character can maintain her husband in competition with the husband of Mrs Banger. I have the honor to propose for your hand.

MRS FARRELL. D'ye mean you want to marry me?

MITCHENER. I do.

MRS FARRELL. No thank you. I'd have to work for you just the same; only I shouldnt get any wages for it.

BALSQUITH. That will be remedied when women get the vote. Ive had to promise that.

MITCHENER [*winningly*] Mrs Farrell: you have been charwoman here now ever since I took up my duties. Have you really never, in your more romantic moments, cast a favorable eye on my person?

MRS FARRELL. Ive been too busy casting an unfavorable eye on your cloze an on the litther you make with your papers.

MITCHENER [*wounded*] Am I to understand that you refuse me?

MRS FARRELL. Just wait a bit. [*She takes Mitchener's chair and rings up the telephone*] Double three oh seven Elephant.

MITCHENER. I trust youre not ringing for the police, Mrs Farrell. I assure you I'm perfectly sane.

MRS FARRELL [*into the telephone*] Is that you, Eliza? [*She listens for the answer*]. Not out o bed yet! Go and pull her out be the heels, the lazy sthreel; an tell her her mother wants to speak to her very particularly about General Mitchener. [*To Mitchener*] Dont you be afeard: I know youre sane enough when youre not talkin about the Germans. [*Into the telephone*] Is that you, Eliza? [*She listens for the answer*]. D'ye remember me givin you a clout on the side of the head for tellin me that if I only knew how to play me cards I could marry any General on the staff instead o disgracin you be bein a charwoman? [*She listens for the answer*]. Well, I can have General Mitchener without playin any cards at all. What d'ye think I ought to say? [*She listens*]. Well, I'm no chicken meself. [*To Mitchener*] How old are you?

MITCHENER [*with an effort*] Fifty-two.

MRS FARRELL [*into the telephone*] He says he's fifty-two. [*She listens; then, to Mitchener*] She says youre down in Who's Who as sixty-one.

MITCHENER. Damn Who's Who!

MRS FARRELL [*into the telephone*] Anyhow I wouldnt let that stand in the way. [*She listens*]. If I really what? [*She listens*]. I cant hear you. If I really what? [*She listens*]. Who druv him? I never said a word to— Eh? [*She listens*]. Oh, love him. Arra, dont be a fool, child. [*To Mitchener*] She wants to know do I really love you. [*Into the telephone*] It's likely indeed I'd frighten the man off with any such nonsense at my age. What? [*She listens*]. Well, thats just what I was thinkin.

MITCHENER. May I ask what you were thinking, Mrs Farrell? This suspense is awful.

MRS FARRELL. I was thinkin that praps the Duchess might like her daughther-in-law's mother to be a General's lady betther than to be a charwoman. [*Into the telephone*] Waitle youre married yourself, me fine lady: youll find out that every woman's a charwoman from the day she's married. [*She listens*]. Then you think I might take him? [*She listens*]. G'lang, you young scald: if I had you here I'd teach you manners. [*She listens*]. Thats enough now. Back wid you to bed; and be thankful I'm not there to put me slipper across you. [*She rings off*]. The impudence! [*To Mitchener*] Bless you, me childher, may you be happy, she says. [*To Balsquith, going to his side of the room*] Give dear old Mitch me love, she says.

The Orderly opens the door, ushering in Lady Corinthia.

THE ORDERLY. Lady Corinthia Fanshawe to speak to you, sir.

LADY CORINTHIA. General Mitchener: your designs on Mrs Banger are defeated. She is engaged to General Sandstone. Do you still prefer her to me?

MRS FARRELL. He's out o the hunt. He's engaged to me.

The Orderly, overcome by this news, reels from the door to the standing desk and clutches the stool to save himself from collapsing.

MITCHENER. And extremely proud of it, Lady Corinthia.

LADY CORINTHIA [*contemptuously*] She suits you exactly. [*Coming to Balsquith*] Mr Balsquith: you, at least, are not a Philistine.

BALSQUITH. No, Lady Corinthia; but I'm a confirmed bachelor. I dont want a wife; but I want an Egeria.

MRS FARRELL. More shame for you!

LADY CORINTHIA. Silence, woman. The position and functions of a wife may suit your gross nature. An Egeria is exactly what I desire to be. [*To Balsquith*] Can you play accompaniments?

BALSQUITH. Melodies only, I regret to say. With one finger. But my brother, who is a very obliging fellow, and not unlike me personally, is acquainted with three chords, with which he manages to accompany most of the comic songs of the day.

LADY CORINTHIA. I do not sing comic songs. Neither will you when I am your Egeria. You must come to my musical at-home this afternoon. I will allow you to sit at my feet.

BALSQUITH [*doing so*] That is my ideal of romantic happiness. It commits me exactly as far as I desire to venture. Thank you.

THE ORDERLY. Wot price me, General? Wont you celebrate your engagement by doin somethin for me? Maynt I be promoted to be a sergeant?

MITCHENER. Youre too utterly incompetent to discharge the duties of a sergeant. You are only fit to be a lieutenant. I shall recommend you for a commission.

THE ORDERLY. Hooray! The Parkinsons o Stepney'll be proud to have me call on em now. I'll go and tell the sergeant what I think of him. Hooray! [*He rushes out*].

MRS FARRELL [*going to the door and calling after him*] You might have the manners to shut the door afther you. [*She shuts it and comes between Mitchener and Lady Corinthia*].

MITCHENER. Poor wretch! the day after civil rights are conceded to the army he and Chubbs-Jenkinson will be found incapable of maintaining discipline. They will be sacked and replaced by really capable men. Mrs Farrell: as we are engaged, and I am anxious to do the correct thing in every way, I am quite willing to kiss you if you wish it.

MRS FARRELL. Youd only feel like a fool; and so would I.

MITCHENER. You are really the most sensible woman. Ive made an extremely wise choice. [*He kisses her hand*].

LADY CORINTHIA [*to Balsquith*] You may kiss my hand, if you wish.

BALSQUITH [*cautiously*] I think we had better not commit ourselves too far. Let us change a subject which threatens to become embarrassing. [*To Mitchener*] The moral of the occasion for you, Mitchener, appears to be that youve got to give up treating soldiers as if they were schoolboys.

MITCHENER. The moral for you, Balsquith, is that youve got to give up treating women as if they were angels. Ha ha!

MRS FARRELL. It's a mercy youve found one another out at last. Thats enough now.

THE GLIMPSE OF REALITY

A TRAGEDIETTA

THE GLIMPSE OF REALITY

A TRAGEDIETTA

In the fifteenth century A.D. Gloaming. An inn on the edge of an Italian lake. A stone cross with a pedestal of steps. A very old friar sitting on the steps. The angelus rings. The friar prays and crosses himself. A girl ferries a boat to the shore and comes up the bank to the cross.

THE GIRL. Father: were you sent here by a boy from—

THE FRIAR [*in a high, piping, but clear voice*] I'm a very old man. Oh, very old. Old enough to be your great grandfather, my daughter. Oh, very very old.

THE GIRL. But were you sent here by a boy from—

THE FRIAR. Oh yes, yes, yes, yes, yes. Quite a boy, he was. Very young. And I'm very old. Oh, very very old, dear daughter.

THE GIRL. Are you a holy man?

THE FRIAR [*ecstatically*] Oh, very holy. Very, very, very, very holy.

THE GIRL. But have you your wits still about you, father? Can you absolve me from a great sin?

THE FRIAR. Oh yes, yes, yes. A very great sin. I'm very old; but Ive my wits about me. I'm one hundred and thirteen years old, by the grace of Our Lady; but I still remember all my Latin; and I can bind and loose; and I'm very very wise; for I'm old and have left far behind me the world, the flesh, and the devil. You see I am blind, daughter; but when a boy told me that there was a duty for me to do here, I came without a guide, straight to this spot, led by St Barbara. She led me to this stone, daughter. It's a comfortable stone to me: she has blessed it for me.

THE GIRL. It's a cross, father.

THE FRIAR [*piping rapturously*] Oh blessed, blessed, ever blessed be my holy patroness for leading me to this sacred spot. Is there any building near this, daughter? The boy mentioned an inn.

THE GIRL. There is an inn, father, not twenty yards away. It's kept by my father, Squarcio.

THE FRIAR. And is there a barn where a very very old man may sleep and have a handful of peas for his supper?

THE GIRL. There is bed and board both for holy men who will take the guilt of our sins from us. Swear to me on the cross that you are a very holy man.

THE FRIAR. I'll do better than that, daughter. I'll prove my holiness to you by a miracle.

THE GIRL. A miracle!

THE FRIAR. A most miraculous miracle. A wonderful miracle! When I was only eighteen years of age I was already famous for my devoutness. When the hand of the blessed Saint Barbara, which was chopped off in the days when the church was persecuted, was found at Viterbo, I was selected by the Pope himself to carry it to Rome for that blessed lady's festival there; and since that my hand has never grown old. It remains young and warm and plump whilst the rest of my body is withered almost to dust, and my voice is cracked and become the whistling you now hear.

THE GIRL. Is that true? Let me see. [*He takes her hand in his. She kneels and kisses it fervently*] Oh, it's true. You are a saint. Heaven has sent you in answer to my prayer.

THE FRIAR. As soft as your neck, is it not? [*He caresses her neck*].

THE GIRL. It thrills me: it is wonderful.

THE FRIAR. It thrills me also, daughter. That, too, is a miracle at my age.

THE GIRL. Father—

THE FRIAR. Come closer, daughter. I'm very very old and very very very deaf: you must speak quite close to my ear if you speak low. [*She kneels with her breast against his arm and her chin on his shoulder*]. Good. Good. Thats better. Oh, I'm very very old.

THE GIRL. Father: I am about to commit a deadly sin.

THE FRIAR. Do, my daughter. Do, do, do, do, do.

THE GIRL [*discouraged*] Oh, you do not hear what I say.

THE FRIAR. Not hear! Then come closer, daughter. Oh, much

much closer. Put your arm round my shoulders, and speak in my ear. Do not be ashamed, my daughter: I'm only a sack of old bones. You can hear them rattle. [*He shakes his shoulders and makes the beads of his rosary rattle at the same time*]. Listen to the old man's bones rattling. Oh, take the old old man to heaven, Blessed Barbara.

THE GIRL. Your wits are wandering. Listen to me. Are you listening?

THE FRIAR. Yes yes yes yes yes yes yes. Remember: whether I hear or not, I can absolve. All the better for you perhaps if I do not hear the worst. He! He! He! Well well. When my wits wander, squeeze my young hand; and the blessed Barbara will restore my faculties. [*She squeezes his hand vigorously*]. Thats right. Tha-a-a-ats right. Now I remember what I am and who you are. Proceed, my child.

THE GIRL. Father, I am to be married this year to a young fisherman.

THE FRIAR. The devil you are, my dear.

THE GIRL [*squeezing his hand*] Oh listen, listen; you are wandering again.

THE FRIAR. Thats right: hold my hand tightly. I understand, I understand. This young fisherman is neither very beautiful nor very brave; but he is honest and devoted to you; and there is something about him different to all the other young men.

THE GIRL. You know him, then!

THE FRIAR. No no no no no. I'm too old to remember people. But Saint Barbara tells me everything.

THE GIRL. Then you know why we cant marry yet.

THE FRIAR. He is too poor. His mother will not let him unless his bride has a dowry—

THE GIRL [*interrupting him impetuously*] Yes, yes: oh blessed be Saint Barbara for sending you to me! Thirty crowns—thirty crowns from a poor girl like me: it is wicked—monstrous. I must sin to earn it.

THE FRIAR. That will not be your sin, but his mother's.

THE GIRL. Oh, that is true: I never thought of that. But will she suffer for it?

THE FRIAR. Thousands of years in purgatory for it, my daughter. The worse the sin, the longer she will suffer. So let her have it as hot as possible. [*The girl recoils*]. Do not let go my hand: I'm wandering. [*She squeezes his hand*]. Thats right, darling. Sin is a very wicked thing, my daughter. Even a mother-in-law's sin is very expensive; for your husband would stint you to pay for masses for her soul.

THE GIRL. That is true. You are very wise, father.

THE FRIAR. Let it be a venial sin: an amiable sin. What sin were you thinking of, for instance?

THE GIRL. There is a young Count Ferruccio [*the Friar starts at the name*], son of the tyrant of Parma—

THE FRIAR. An excellent young man, daughter. You could not sin with a more excellent young man. But thirty crowns is too much to ask from him. He cant afford it. He is a beggar: an outcast. He made love to Madonna Brigita, the sister of Cardinal Poldi, a Cardinal eighteen years of age, a nephew of the Holy Father. The Cardinal surprised Ferruccio with his sister; and Ferruccio's temper got the better of him. He threw that holy young Cardinal out of the window and broke his arm.

THE GIRL. You know everything.

THE FRIAR. Saint Barbara, my daughter, Saint Barbara. *I* know nothing. But where have you seen Ferruccio? Saint Barbara says that he never saw you in his life, and has not thirty crowns in the world.

THE GIRL. Oh, why does not Saint Barbara tell you that I am an honest girl who would not sell herself for a thousand crowns.

THE FRIAR. Do not give way to pride, daughter. Pride is one of the seven deadly sins.

THE GIRL. I know that, father; and believe me, I'm humble and good. I swear to you by Our Lady that it is not Ferruccio's love that I must take, but his life. [*The Friar, startled, turns powerfully on her*]. Do not be angry, dear father: do not cast me off. What is a poor girl to do? We are very poor, my father and I. And I am not to kill him. I am only to decoy him here; for he is a devil for women; and once he is in the inn, my father will do the rest.

THE FRIAR. [*in a rich baritone voice*] Will he, by thunder and lightning and the flood and all the saints, will he? [*He flings off his gown and beard, revealing himself as a handsome youth, a nobleman by his dress, as he springs up and rushes to the door of the inn, which he batters with a stone*]. Ho there, Squarcio, rascal, assassin, son of a pig: come out that I may break every bone in your carcass.

THE GIRL. You are a young man!

THE FRIAR. Another miracle of Saint Barbara. [*Kicking the door*] Come out, whelp: come out, rat. Come out and be killed. Come out and be beaten to a jelly. Come out, dog, swine, animal, mangy hound, lousy— [*Squarcio comes out, sword in hand*]. Do you know who I am, dog?

SQUARCIO [*impressed*] No, your Excellency.

THE FRIAR. I am Ferruccio, Count Ferruccio, the man you are to kill, the man your devil of a daughter is to decoy, the man who is now going to cut you into forty thousand pieces and throw you into the lake.

SQUARCIO. Keep your temper, Signor Count.

FERRUCCIO. I'll not keep my temper. Ive an uncontrollable temper. I get blinding splitting headaches if I do not relieve my temper by acts of violence. I'll relieve it now by pounding you to jelly, assassin that you are.

SQUARCIO [*shrugging his shoulders*] As you please, Signor Count. I may as well earn my money now as another time. [*He handles his sword*].

FERRUCCIO. Ass: do you suppose I have trusted myself in this territory without precautions? My father has made a wager with your feudal lord here about me.

SQUARCIO. What wager, may it please your Excellency?

FERRUCCIO. What wager, blockhead! Why, that if I am assassinated, the murderer will not be brought to justice.

SQUARCIO. So that if I kill you—

FERRUCCIO. Your Baron will lose ten crowns unless you are broken on the wheel for it.

SQUARCIO. Only ten crowns, Excellency! Your father does not value your life very highly.

FERRUCCIO. Dolt. Can you not reason? If the sum were larger your Baron would win it by killing me himself and breaking somebody else on the wheel for it: you, most likely. Ten crowns is just enough to make him break you on the wheel if you kill me, but not enough to pay for all the masses that would have to be said for him if the guilt were his.

SQUARCIO. That is very clever, Excellency. [*Sheathing his sword*]. You shall not be slain: I will take care of that. If anything happens, it will be an accident.

FERRUCCIO. Body of Bacchus! I forgot that trick. I should have killed you when my blood was hot.

SQUARCIO. Will your Excellency please to step in? My best room and my best cooking are at your Excellency's disposal.

FERRUCCIO. To the devil with your mangy kennel! You want to tell every traveller that Count Ferruccio slept in your best bed and was eaten by your army of fleas. Take yourself out of my sight when you have told me where the next inn is.

SQUARCIO. I'm sorry to thwart your Excellency; but I have not forgotten your father's wager; and until you leave this territory I shall stick to you like your shadow.

FERRUCCIO. And why, pray?

SQUARCIO. Someone else might kill your Excellency; and, as you say, my illustrious Baron might break me on the wheel for your father's ten crowns. I must protect your Excellency, whether your Excellency is willing or not.

FERRUCCIO. If you dare to annoy me, I'll handle your bones so that there will be nothing left for the hangman to break. Now what do you say?

SQUARCIO. I say that your Excellency over-rates your Excellency's strength. You would have no more chance against me than a grasshopper. [*Ferruccio makes a demonstration*]. Oh, I know that your Excellency has been taught by fencers and wrestlers and the like; but I can take all you can give me without turning a hair, and settle the account when you are out of breath.

That is why common men are dangerous, your Excellency: they are inured to toil and endurance. Besides, I know all the tricks.

THE GIRL. Do not attempt to quarrel with my father, Count. It must be as he says. It is his profession to kill. What could you do against him? If you want to beat somebody, you must beat me. [*She goes into the inn*].

SQUARCIO. I advise you not to try that, Excellency. She also is very strong.

FERRUCCIO. Then I shall have a headache: thats all. [*He throws himself ill-humoredly on a bench at the table outside the inn. Giulia returns with a tablecloth and begins preparing the table for a meal*].

SQUARCIO. A good supper, Excellency, will prevent that. And Giulia will sing for you.

FERRUCCIO. Not while theres a broomstick in the house to break her ugly head with. Do you suppose I'm going to listen to the howling of a she-wolf who wanted me to absolve her for getting me killed?

SQUARCIO. The poor must live as well as the rich, sir. Giulia is a good girl. [*He goes into the inn*].

FERRUCCIO [*shouting after him*] Must the rich die that the poor may live?

GIULIA. The poor often die that the rich may live.

FERRUCCIO. What an honor for them! But it would have been no honor for me to die merely that you might marry your clod of a fisherman.

GIULIA. You are spiteful, Signor.

FERRUCCIO. I am no troubadour, Giuliaccia, if that is what you mean.

GIULIA. How did you know about my Sandro and his mother? How were you so wise when you pretended to be an old friar? you that are so childish now that you are yourself?

FERRUCCIO. I take it that either Saint Barbara inspired me, or else that you are a great fool.

GIULIA. Saint Barbara will surely punish you for that wicked lie you told about her hand.

FERRUCCIO. The hand that thrilled you?

GIULIA. That was blasphemy. You should not have done it. You made me feel as if I had had a taste of heaven; and then you poisoned it in my heart as a taste of hell. That was wicked and cruel. You nobles are cruel.

FERRUCCIO. Well! do you expect us to nurse your babies for you? Our work is to rule and to fight. Ruling is nothing but inflicting cruelties on wrongdoers: fighting is nothing but being cruel to one's enemies. You poor people leave us all the cruel work, and then wonder that we are cruel. Where would you be if we left it undone? Outside the life I lead all to myself—the life of thought and poetry—I know only two pleasures: cruelty and lust. I desire revenge: I desire women. And both of them disappoint me when I get them.

GIULIA. It would have been a good deed to kill you, I think.

FERRUCCIO. Killing is always sport, my Giuliaccia.

SANDRO'S VOICE [*on the lake*] Giulietta! Giulietta!

FERRUCCIO [*calling to him*] Stop that noise. Your Giulietta is here with a young nobleman. Come up and amuse him. [*To Giulietta*] What will you give me if I tempt him to defy his mother and marry you without a dowry?

GIULIA. You are tempting me. A poor girl can give no more than she has. I should think you were a devil if you were not a noble, which is worse. [*She goes out to meet Sandro*].

FERRUCCIO [*calling after her*] The devil does evil for pure love of it: he does not ask a price: he offers it. [*Squarcio returns*]. Prepare supper for four, bandit.

SQUARCIO. Is your appetite so great in this heat, Signor?

FERRUCCIO. There will be four to supper. You, I, your daughter, and Sandro. Do not stint yourselves: I pay for all. Go and prepare more food.

SQUARCIO. Your order is already obeyed, Excellency.

FERRUCCIO. How?

SQUARCIO. I prepared for four, having you here to pay. The only difference your graciousness makes is that we shall have the honor to eat with you instead of after you.

FERRUCCIO. Dog of a bandit: you should have been born a

nobleman.

SQUARCIO. I was born noble, Signor; but as we had no money to maintain our pretensions, I dropped them. [*He goes back into the inn*].

Giulia returns with Sandro.

GIULIA. This is the lad, Excellency. Sandro: this is his lordship Count Ferruccio.

SANDRO. At your lordship's service.

FERRUCCIO. Sit down, Sandro. You, Giulia, and Squarcio are my guests. [*They sit*].

GIULIA. Ive told Sandro everything, Excellency.

FERRUCCIO. And what does Sandro say? [*Squarcio returns with a tray*].

GIULIA. He says that if you have ten crowns in your purse, and we kill you, we can give them to the Baron. It would be the same to him as if he got it from your illustrious father.

SQUARCIO. Stupid: the Count is cleverer than you think. No matter how much money you give the Baron he can always get ten crowns more by breaking me on the wheel if the Count is killed.

GIULIA. That is true. Sandro did not think of that.

SANDRO [*with cheerful politeness*] Oh! what a head I have! I am not clever, Excellency. At the same time you must know that I did not mean my Giulietta to tell you. I know my duty to your Excellency better than that.

FERRUCCIO. Come! You are dear people: charming people. Let us get to work at the supper. You shall be the mother of the family and give us our portions, Giulietta. [*They take their places*]. Thats right. Serve me last, Giulietta. Sandro is hungry.

SQUARCIO [*to the girl*] Come come! do you not see that his Excellency will touch nothing until we have had some first. [*He eats*]. See, Excellency! I have tasted everything. To tell you the truth, poisoning is an art I do not understand.

FERRUCCIO. Very few professional poisoners do, Squarcio. One of the best professionals in Rome poisoned my uncle and aunt. They are alive still. The poison cured my uncle's gout, and only made my aunt thin, which was exactly what she desired, poor lady, as she was losing her figure terribly.

SQUARCIO. There is nothing like the sword, Excellency.

SANDRO. Except the water, Father Squarcio. Trust a fisherman to know that. Nobody can tell that drowning was not an accident.

FERRUCCIO. What does Giulietta say?

GIULIA. I should not kill a man if I hated him. You cannot torment a man when he is dead. Men kill because they think it is what they call a satisfaction. But that is only fancy.

FERRUCCIO. And if you loved him? Would you kill him then?

GIULIA. Perhaps. If you love a man you are his slave: everything he says—everything he does—is a stab to your heart: every day is a long dread of losing him. Better kill him if there be no other escape.

FERRUCCIO. How well you have brought up your family, Squarcio! Some more omelette, Sandro?

SANDRO [*very cheerfully*] I thank your Excellency. [*He accepts and eats with an appetite*].

FERRUCCIO. I pledge you all. To the sword and the fisherman's net: to love and hate! [*He drinks: they drink with him*].

SQUARCIO. To the sword!

SANDRO. To the net, Excellency, with thanks for the honor.

GIULIA. To love, Signor.

FERRUCCIO. To hate: the noble's portion!

SQUARCIO. The meal has done you good, Excellency. How do you feel now?

FERRUCCIO. I feel that there is nothing but a bait of ten crowns between me and death, Squarcio.

SQUARCIO. It is enough, Excellency. And enough is always enough.

SANDRO. Do not think of that, Excellency. It is only that we are poor folk, and have to consider how to make both ends meet as one may say. [*Looking at the dish*] Excellency—?

FERRUCCIO. Finish it, Sandro. Ive done.

SANDRO. Father Squarcio?

SQUARCIO. Finish it, finish it.

SANDRO. Giulietta?

GIULIA [*surprised*] Me? Oh no. Finish it, Sandro: it will only go to the pig.

SANDRO. Then, with your Excellency's permission—[*he helps himself*].

SQUARCIO. Sing for his Excellency, my daughter.

Giulia turns to the door to fetch her mandoline.

FERRUCCIO. I shall jump into the lake, Squarcio, if your cat begins to miaowl.

SANDRO [*always cheerful and reassuring*] No, no, Excellency: Giulietta sings very sweetly: have no fear.

FERRUCCIO. I do not care for singing: at least not the singing of peasants. There is only one thing for which one woman will do as well as another, and that is lovemaking. Come, Father Squarcio: I will buy Giulietta from you: you can have her back for nothing when I am tired of her. How much?

SQUARCIO. In ready money, or in promises?

FERRUCCIO. Old fox. Ready money.

SQUARCIO. Fifty crowns, Excellency.

FERRUCCIO. Fifty crowns! Fifty crowns for that black-faced devil! I would not give fifty crowns for one of my mother's ladies-in-waiting. Fifty pence, you must mean.

SQUARCIO. Doubtless your Excellency, being a younger son, is poor. Shall we say five and twenty crowns?

FERRUCCIO. I tell you she is not worth five.

SQUARCIO. Oh, if you come to what she is worth, Excellency, what are any of us worth? I take it that you are a gentleman, not a merchant.

GIULIA. What are you worth, Signorino?

FERRUCCIO. I am accustomed to be asked for favors, Giuliaccia, not to be asked impertinent questions.

GIULIA. What would you do if a strong man took you by the scruff of your neck, or his daughter thrust a knife in your throat, Signor?

FERRUCCIO. It would be many a year, my gentle Giuliaccia, before any baseborn man or woman would dare threaten a nobleman again. The whole village would be flayed alive.

SANDRO. Oh no, Signor. These things often have a great air of being accidents. And the great families are well content that they should appear so. It is such a great trouble to flay a whole village alive. Here by the water, accidents are so common.

SQUARCIO. We of the nobility, Signor, are not strict enough. I learnt that when I took to breeding horses. The horses you breed from thoroughbreds are not all worth the trouble: most of them are screws. Well, the horsebreeder gets rid of his screws for what they will fetch: they go to labor like any peasant's beast. But our nobility does not study its business so carefully. If you are a screw, and the son of a baron, you are brought up to think yourself a little god, though you are nothing, and cannot rule yourself, much less a province. And you presume, and presume, and presume—

GIULIA. And insult, and insult, and insult.

SQUARCIO. Until one day you find yourself in a strange place with nothing to help you but your own hands and your own wits—

GIULIA. And you perish—

SANDRO. Accidentally—

GIULIA. And your soul goes crying to your father for vengeance—

SQUARCIO. If indeed, my daughter, there be any soul left when the body is slain.

FERRUCCIO [crossing himself hastily] Dog of a bandit: do you dare doubt the existence of God and the soul?

SQUARCIO. I think, Excellency, that the soul is so precious a gift that God will not give it to a man for nothing. He must earn if by being something and doing something. I should not like to kill a man with a good soul. Ive had a dog that had, I'm persuaded, made itself something of a soul; and if anyone had murdered that dog, I would have slain him. But shew me a man with no soul: one who has never done anything or been anything; and I will kill him for ten crowns with as little remorse as I would stick a pig.

SANDRO. Unless he be a nobleman, of course—

SQUARCIO. In which case the price is fifty crowns.

FERRUCCIO. Soul or no soul?

SQUARCIO. When it comes to a matter of fifty crowns, Excellency, business is business. The man who pays me must square the account with the devil. It is for my employer to consider whether the action be a good one or no: it is for me to earn his money honestly. When I said I should not like to kill a man with a good soul, I meant killing on my own account: not professionally.

FERRUCCIO. Are you such a fool then as to spoil your own trade by sometimes killing people for nothing?

SQUARCIO. One kills a snake for nothing, Excellency. One kills a dog for nothing sometimes.

SANDRO [*apologetically*] Only a mad dog, Excellency, of course.

SQUARCIO. A pet dog, too. One that eats and eats and is useless, and makes an honest man's house dirty. [*He rises*]. Come, Sandro, and help me to clean up. You, Giulia, stay and entertain his Excellency.

He and Sandro make a hammock of the cloth, in which they carry the wooden platters and fragments of the meal indoors. Ferruccio is left alone with Giulia. The gloaming deepens.

FERRUCCIO. Does your father do the house work with a great girl like you idling about? Squarcio is a fool, after all.

GIULIA. No, Signor: he has left me here to prevent you from escaping.

FERRUCCIO. There is nothing to be gained by killing me, Giuliaccia.

GIULIA. Perhaps; but I do not know. I saw Sandro make a sign to my father: that is why they went in. Sandro has something in his head.

FERRUCCIO [*brutally*] Lice, no doubt.

GIULIA [*unmoved*] That would only make him scratch his head, Signor, not make signs with it to my father. You did wrong to throw the Cardinal out of the window.

FERRUCCIO. Indeed: and pray why?

GIULIA. He will pay thirty crowns for your dead body. Then Sandro could marry me.

FERRUCCIO. And be broken on the wheel for it.

GIULIA. It would look like an accident, Signor. Sandro is very clever; and he is so humble and cheerful and good-tempered that people do not suspect him as they suspect my father.

FERRUCCIO. Giulietta: if I reach Sacromonte in safety, I swear to send you thirty crowns by a sure messenger within ten days. Then you can marry your Sandro. How does that appeal to you?

GIULIA. Your oath is not worth twenty pence, Signor.

FERRUCCIO. Do you think I will die here like a rat in a trap— [his breath fails him].

GIULIA. Rats have to wait in their traps for death, Signor. Why not you?

FERRUCCIO. I'll fight.

GIULIA. You are welcome, Signor. The blood flows freeest when it is hot.

FERRUCCIO. She devil! Listen to me, Giulietta—

GIULIA. It is useless, Signor. Giulietta or Giuliaccia: it makes no difference. If they two in there kill you it will be no more to me—except for the money—than if my father trod on a snail.

FERRUCCIO. Oh, it is not possible that I, a nobleman, should die by such filthy hands.

GIULIA. You have lived by them, Signor. I see no sign of any work on your own hands. We can bring death as well as life, we poor people, Signor.

FERRUCCIO. Mother of God, what shall I do?

GIULIA. Pray, Signor.

FERRUCCIO. Pray! With the taste of death in my mouth? I can think of nothing.

GIULIA. It is only that you have forgotten your beads, Signor [she picks up the Friar's rosary]. You remember the old man's bones rattling. Here they are [she rattles them before him].

FERRUCCIO. That reminds me. I know of a painter in the north that can paint such beautiful saints that the heart goes out of one's body to look at them. If I get out of this alive I'll make him paint

St Barbara so that every one can see that she is lovelier than St Cecilia, who looks like my washerwoman's mother in her Chapel in our cathedral. Can you give St Cecilia a picture if she lets me be killed?

GIULIA. No; but I can give her many prayers.

FERRUCCIO. Prayers cost nothing. She will prefer the picture unless she is a greater fool than I take her to be.

GIULIA. She will thank the painter for it, not you, Signor. And I'll tell her in my prayers to appear to the painter in a vision, and order him to paint her just as he sees her if she really wishes to be painted.

FERRUCCIO. You are devilishly ready with your answers. Tell me, Giulietta: is what your father told me true? Is your blood really noble?

GIULIA. It is red, Signor, like the blood of the Christ in the picture in Church. I do not know if yours is different. I shall see when my father kills you.

FERRUCCIO. Do you know what I am thinking, Giulietta?

GIULIA. No, Signor.

FERRUCCIO. I am thinking that if the good God would oblige me by taking my fool of an elder brother up to heaven, and his silly doll of a wife with him before she has time to give him a son, you would make a rare duchess for me. Come! Will you help me to outwit your father and Sandro if I marry you afterwards?

GIULIA. No, Signor: I'll help them to kill you.

FERRUCCIO. My back is to the wall, then?

GIULIA. To the precipice, I think, Signor.

FERRUCCIO. No matter, so my face is to the danger. Did you notice, Giulia, a minute ago? I was frightened.

GIULIA. Yes, Signor. I saw it in your face.

FERRUCCIO. The terror of terrors.

GIULIA. The terror of death.

FERRUCCIO. No: death is nothing. I can face a stab just as I faced having my tooth pulled out at Faenza.

GIULIA [shuddering with sincere sympathy] Poor Signorino!

That must have hurt horribly.

FERRUCCIO. What! You pity me for the tooth affair, and you did not pity me in that hideous agony of terror that is not the terror of death nor of anything else, but pure grim terror in itself.

GIULIA. It was the terror of the soul, Signor. And I do not pity your soul: you have a wicked soul. But you have pretty teeth.

FERRUCCIO. The toothache lasted a week; but the agony of my soul was too dreadful to last five minutes: I should have died of it if it could have kept its grip of me. But you helped me out of it.

GIULIA. I, Signor!

FERRUCCIO. Yes: you. If you had pitied me: if you had been less inexorable than death itself, I should have broken down and cried and begged for mercy. But now I have come up against something hard: something real: something that does not care for me. I see now the truth of my excellent uncle's opinion that I was a spoilt cub. When I wanted anything I threatened men or ran crying to women; and they gave it to me. I dreamed and romanced: imagining things as I wanted them, not as they really are. There is nothing like a good look into the face of death: close up: right on you: for shewing you how little you really believe and how little you really are. A priest said to me once, "In your last hour everything will fall away from you except your religion." But I have lived through my last hour; and my religion was the first thing that fell away from me. When I was forced at last to believe in grim death I knew at last what belief was, and that I had never believed in anything before: I had only flattered myself with pretty stories, and sheltered myself behind Mumbo Jumbo, as a soldier will shelter himself from arrows behind a clump of thistles that only hide the shooters from him. When I believe in everything that is real as I believed for that moment in death, then I shall be a man at last. I have tasted the water of life from the cup of death; and it may be now that my real life began with this [*he holds up the rosary*] and will end with the triple crown or the heretic's fire: I care not which. [*Springing to his feet*] Come out, then, dog of a bandit, and fight a man who has found his soul. [*Squarcio appears at the door, sword in hand.*

Ferruccio leaps at him and strikes him full in the chest with his dagger. Squarcio puts back his left foot to brace himself against the shock. The dagger snaps as if it had struck a stone wall].

GIULIA. Quick, Sandro.

Sandro, who has come stealing round the corner of the inn with a fishing net, casts it over Ferruccio, and draws it tight.

SQUARCIO. Your Excellency will excuse my shirt of mail. A good home blow, nevertheless, Excellency.

SANDRO. Your Excellency will excuse my net: it is a little damp.

FERRUCCIO. Well, what now? Accidental drowning, I suppose.

SANDRO. Eh, Excellency, it is such a pity to throw a good fish back into the water when once you have got him safe in your net. My Giulietta: hold the net for me.

GIULIA [*taking the net and twisting it in her hands to draw it tighter round him*] I have you very fast now, Signorino, like a little bird in a cage.

FERRUCCIO. You have my body, Giulia. My soul is free.

GIULIA. Is it, Signor? I think Saint Barbara has got that in her net too. She has turned your jest into earnest.

SANDRO. It is indeed true, sir, that those who come under the special protection of God and the Saints are always a little mad; and this makes us think it very unlucky to kill a madman. And since from what Father Squarcio and I overheard, it is clear that your Excellency, though a very wise and reasonable young gentleman in a general way, is somewhat cracked on the subject of the soul and so forth, we have resolved to see that no harm comes to your Excellency.

FERRUCCIO. As you please. My life is only a drop falling from the vanishing clouds to the everlasting sea, from finite to infinite, and itself part of the infinite.

SANDRO [*impressed*] Your Excellency speaks like a crazy but very holy book. Heaven forbid that we should raise a hand against you? But your Excellency will notice that this good action will cost us thirty crowns.

FERRUCCIO. Is it not worth it?

SANDRO. Doubtless, doubtless. It will in fact save us the price of certain masses which we should otherwise have had said for the souls of certain persons who—ahem! Well, no matter. But we think it dangerous and unbecoming that a nobleman like your Excellency should travel without a retinue, and unarmed; for your dagger is unfortunately broken, Excellency. If you would therefore have the condescension to accept Father Squarcio as your man-at-arms—your servant in all but the name, to save his nobility—he will go with you to any town in which you will feel safe from His Eminence the Cardinal, and will leave it to your Excellency's graciousness as to whether his magnanimous conduct will not then deserve some trifling present: say a wedding gift for my Giulietta.

FERRUCCIO. Good: the man I tried to slay will save me from being slain. Who would have thought Saint Barbara so full of irony!

SANDRO. And if the offer your Excellency was good enough to make in respect of Giulietta still stands—

FERRUCCIO. Rascal: have you then no soul?

SANDRO. I am a poor man, Excellency: I cannot afford these luxuries of the rich.

FERRUCCIO. There is a certain painter will presently make a great picture of St Barbara; and Giulia will be his model. He will pay her well. Giulia: release the bird. It is time for it to fly.

She takes the net from his shoulders.

COOLE PARK, *Summer,* 1909.

PASSION, POISON, AND PETRIFACTION

OR

THE FATAL GAZOGENE

A BRIEF TRAGEDY FOR BARNS AND BOOTHS

THIS tragedy was written at the request of Mr Cyril Maude, under whose direction it was performed repeatedly, with colossal success, in a booth in Regent's Park, for the benefit of The Actors' Orphanage, on the 14th July 1905, by Miss Irene Vanbrugh, Miss Nancy Price, Mr G. P. Huntley, Mr Cyril Maude, Mr Eric Lewis, Mr Arthur Williams, and Mr Lennox Pawle.

As it is extremely difficult to find an actor capable of eating a real ceiling, it will be found convenient in performance to substitute the tops of old wedding cakes for bits of plaster. There is but little difference in material between the two substances; but the taste of the wedding cake is considered more agreeable by many people.

The orchestra should consist of at least a harp, a drum, and a pair of cymbals, these instruments being the most useful in enhancing the stage effect.

The landlord may with equal propriety be a landlady, if that arrangement be better suited to the resources of the company.

As the Bill Bailey song has not proved immortal, any equally appropriate ditty of the moment may be substituted.

PASSION, POISON, AND PETRIFACTION
OR
THE FATAL GAZOGENE

In a bed-sitting room in a fashionable quarter of London a lady sits at her dressing-table, with her maid combing her hair. It is late; and the electric lamps are glowing. Apparently the room is bedless; but there stands against the opposite wall to that at which the dressing-table is placed a piece of furniture that suggests a bookcase without carrying conviction. On the same side is a chest of drawers of that disastrous kind which, recalcitrant to the opener until she is provoked to violence, then suddenly come wholly out and defy all her efforts to fit them in again. Opposite this chest of drawers, on the lady's side of the room, is a cupboard. The presence of a row of gentleman's boots beside the chest of drawers proclaims that the lady is married. Her own boots are beside the cupboard. The third wall is pierced midway by the door, above which is a cuckoo clock. Near the door a pedestal bears a portrait bust of the lady in plaster. There is a fan on the dressing-table, a hatbox and rug strap on the chest of drawers, an umbrella and a bootjack against the wall near the bed. The general impression is one of brightness, beauty, and social ambition, damped by somewhat inadequate means. A certain air of theatricality is produced by the fact that though the room is rectangular it has only three walls. Not a sound is heard except the overture and the crackling of the lady's hair as the maid's brush draws electric sparks from it in the dry air of the London midsummer.

The cuckoo clock strikes sixteen.

THE LADY. How much did the clock strike, Phyllis?

PHYLLIS. Sixteen, my lady.

THE LADY. That means eleven o'clock, does it not?

PHYLLIS. Eleven at night, my lady. In the morning it means half-past two; so if you hear it strike sixteen during your slumbers, do not rise.

THE LADY. I will not, Phyllis. Phyllis: I am weary. I will go to bed. Prepare my couch.

Phyllis crosses the room to the bookcase and touches a button. The front of the bookcase falls out with a crash and becomes a bed. A roll of distant thunder echoes the crash.

PHYLLIS [*shuddering*] It is a terrible night. Heaven help all poor mariners at sea! My master is late. I trust nothing has happened to him. Your bed is ready, my lady.

THE LADY. Thank you, Phyllis. [*She rises and approaches the bed*]. Goodnight.

PHYLLIS. Will your ladyship not undress?

THE LADY. Not tonight, Phyllis. [*Glancing through where the fourth wall is missing*] Not under the circumstances.

PHYLLIS [*impulsively throwing herself on her knees by her mistress's side, and clasping her round the waist*] Oh, my beloved mistress, I know not why or how; but I feel that I shall never see you alive again. There is murder in the air. [*Thunder*]. Hark!

THE LADY. Strange! As I sat there methought I heard angels singing, Oh, wont you come home, Bill Bailey? Why should angels call me Bill Bailey? My name is Magnesia Fitztollemache.

PHYLLIS [*emphasizing the title*] Lady Magnesia Fitztollemache.

LADY MAGNESIA. In case we should never again meet in this world, let us take a last farewell.

PHYLLIS [*embracing her with tears*] My poor murdered angel mistress!

LADY MAGNESIA. In case we should meet again, call me at half-past eleven.

PHYLLIS. I will, I will.

Phyllis withdraws, overcome by emotion. Lady Magnesia switches off the electric light, and immediately hears the angels quite distinctly. They sing Bill Bailey so sweetly that she can attend to nothing else, and forgets to remove even her boots as she draws the coverlet over herself and sinks to sleep, lulled by celestial harmony. A white radiance plays on her pillow, and lights up her beautiful face. But the thunder growls again; and a lurid red glow concentrates itself on the door, which is presently flung open, revealing a saturnine figure in evening dress, partially concealed by a crimson cloak. As he steals to-

wards the bed the unnatural glare in his eyes and the broad-bladed dagger nervously gripped in his right hand bode ill for the sleeping lady. Providentially she sneezes on the very brink of eternity; and the tension of the murderer's nerves is such that he bolts precipitately under the bed at the sudden and startling Atscha! *A dull, heavy, rhythmic thumping—the beating of his heart—betrays his whereabouts. Soon he emerges cautiously and raises his head above the bed coverlet level.*

THE MURDERER. I can no longer cower here listening to the agonized thumpings of my own heart. She but snooze in her sleep. I'll do't. [*He again raises the dagger. The angels sing again. He cowers*] What is this? Has that tune reached Heaven?

LADY MAGNESIA [*waking and sitting up*] My husband! [*All the colors of the rainbow chase one another up his face with ghastly brilliancy*]. Why do you change color? And what on earth are you doing with that dagger?

FITZ [*affecting unconcern, but unhinged*] It is a present for you: a present from mother. Pretty, isnt it? [*he displays it fatuously*].

LADY MAGNESIA. But she promised me a fish slice.

FITZ. This is a combination fish slice and dagger. One day you have salmon for dinner. The next you have a murder to commit. See?

LADY MAGNESIA. My sweet mother-in-law! [*Someone knocks at the door*]. That is Adolphus's knock. [*Fitz's face turns a dazzling green*]. What has happened to your complexion? You have turned green. Now I think of it, you always do when Adolphus is mentioned. Arnt you going to let him in?

FITZ. Certainly not. [*He goes to the door*]. Adolphus: you cannot enter. My wife is undressed and in bed.

LADY MAGNESIA [*rising*] I am not. Come in, Adolphus [*she switches on the electric light*].

ADOLPHUS [*without*] Something most important has happened. I must come in for a moment.

FITZ [*calling to Adolphus*] Something important happened? What is it?

ADOLPHUS [*without*] My new clothes have come home.

FITZ. He says his new clothes have come home.

LADY MAGNESIA [*running to the door and opening it*] Oh, come in, come in. Let me see.

Adolphus Bastable enters. He is in evening dress, made in the latest fashion, with the right half of the coat and the left half of the trousers yellow and the other halves black. His silver-spangled waistcoat has a crimson handkerchief stuck between it and his shirt front.

ADOLPHUS. What do you think of it?

LADY MAGNESIA. It is a dream! a creation! [*she turns him about to admire him*].

ADOLPHUS [*proudly*] I shall never be mistaken for a waiter again.

FITZ. A drink, Adolphus?

ADOLPHUS. Thanks.

Fitztollemache goes to the cupboard and takes out a tray with tumblers and a bottle of whisky. He puts them on the dressing-table.

FITZ. Is the gazogene full?

LADY MAGNESIA. Yes: you put in the powders yourself today.

FITZ [*sardonically*] So I did. The special powders! Ha! ha! ha! ha! ha! [*his face is again strangely variegated*].

LADY MAGNESIA. Your complexion is really going to pieces. Why do you laugh in that silly way at nothing?

FITZ. Nothing! Ha, ha! Nothing! Ha, ha, ha!

ADOLPHUS. I hope, Mr Fitztollemache, you are not laughing at my clothes. I warn you that I am an Englishman. You may laugh at my manners, at my brains, at my national institutions; but if you laugh at my clothes, one of us must die.

Thunder.

FITZ. I laughed but at the irony of Fate [*he takes a gazogene from the cupboard*].

ADOLPHUS [*satisfied*] Oh, that! Oh, yes, of course!

FITZ. Let us drown all unkindness in a loving cup. [*He puts the gazogene on the floor in the middle of the room*]. Pardon the absence of a table: we found it in the way and pawned it. [*He takes the whisky bottle from the dressing-table*].

LADY MAGNESIA. We picnic at home now. It is delightful.

She takes three tumblers from the dressing-table and sits on the

*floor, presiding over the gazogene, with Fitz and Adolphus squatting
on her left and right respectively. Fitz pours whisky into the tumblers.*

FITZ [*as Magnesia is about to squirt soda into his tumbler*] Stay!
No soda for me. Let Adolphus have it all—all. I will take mine
neat.

LADY MAGNESIA [*proffering tumbler to Adolphus*] Pledge me,
Adolphus.

FITZ. Kiss the cup, Magnesia. Pledge her, man. Drink deep.

ADOLPHUS. To Magnesia!

FITZ. To Magnesia! [*The two men drink*] It is done. [*Scrambling
to his feet*] Adolphus: you have but ten minutes to live—if so long.

ADOLPHUS. What mean you?

MAGNESIA [*rising*] My mind misgives me. I have a strange feeling here [*touching her heart*].

ADOLPHUS. So have I, but lower down [*touching his stomach*].
That gazogene is disagreeing with me.

FITZ. It was poisoned!

Sensation.

ADOLPHUS [*rising*] Help! Police!

FITZ. Dastard! you would appeal to the law! Can you not die
like a gentleman?

ADOLPHUS. But so young! when I have only worn my new
clothes once.

MAGNESIA. It is too horrible. [*To Fitz*] Fiend! what drove you
to this wicked deed?

FITZ. Jealousy. You admired his clothes: you did not admire
mine.

ADOLPHUS. My clothes [*his face lights up with heavenly radiance*]!
Have I indeed been found worthy to be the first clothes-martyr?
Welcome, death! Hark! angels call me. [*The celestial choir again
raises its favorite chant. He listens with a rapt expression. Suddenly
the angels sing out of tune; and the radiance on the poisoned man's
face turns a sickly green*] Yah—ah! Oh—ahoo! The gazogene is
disagreeing extremely. Oh! [*he throws himself on the bed, writhing*].

MAGNESIA [*to Fitz*] Monster: what have you done? [*She points
to the distorted figure on the bed*]. That was once a Man, beautiful

195

and glorious. What have you made of it? A writhing, agonized, miserable, moribund worm.

ADOLPHUS [*in a tone of the strongest remonstrance*] Oh, I say! Oh, come! No: look here, Magnesia! Really!

MAGNESIA. Oh, is this a time for petty vanity? Think of your misspent life—

ADOLPHUS [*much injured*] Whose misspent life?

MAGNESIA [*continuing relentlessly*] Look into your conscience: look into your stomach. [*Adolphus collapses in hideous spasms. She turns to Fitz*] And this is your handiwork!

FITZ. Mine is a passionate nature, Magnesia. I must have your undivided love. I must have your love: do you hear? LOVE! LOVE!! LOVE!!! LOVE!!!! LOVE!!!!!

He raves, accompanied by a fresh paroxysm from the victim on the bed.

MAGNESIA [*with sudden resolution*] You shall have it.

FITZ [*enraptured*] Magnesia! I have recovered your love! Oh, how slight appears the sacrifice of this man compared to so glorious a reward! I would poison ten men without a thought of self to gain one smile from you.

ADOLPHUS [*in a broken voice*] Farewell, Magnesia: my last hour is at hand. Farewell, farewell, farewell!

MAGNESIA. At this supreme moment, George Fitztollemache, I solemnly dedicate to you all that I formerly dedicated to poor Adolphus.

ADOLPHUS. Oh, please not poor Adolphus yet. I still live, you know.

MAGNESIA. The vital spark but flashes before it vanishes. [*Adolphus groans*]. And now, Adolphus, take this last comfort from the unhappy Magnesia Fitztollemache. As I have dedicated to George all that I gave to you, so I will bury in your grave—or in your urn if you are cremated—all that I gave to him.

FITZ. I hardly follow this.

MAGNESIA. I will explain. George: hitherto I have given Adolphus all the romance of my nature—all my love—all my dreams—all my caresses. Henceforth they are yours!

FITZ. Angel!

MAGNESIA. Adolphus: forgive me if this pains you.

ADOLPHUS. Dont mention it. I hardly feel it. The gazogene is so much worse. [*Taken bad again*] Oh!

MAGNESIA. Peace, poor sufferer: there is still some balm. You are about to hear what I am going to dedicate to you.

ADOLPHUS. All I ask is a peppermint lozenge, for mercy's sake.

MAGNESIA. I have something far better than any lozenge: the devotion of a lifetime. Formerly it was George's. I kept his house, or rather, his lodgings. I mended his clothes. I darned his socks. I bought his food. I interviewed his creditors. I stood between him and the servants. I administered his domestic finances. When his hair needed cutting or his countenance was imperfectly washed, I pointed it out to him. The trouble that all this gave me made him prosaic in my eyes. Familiarity bred contempt. Now all that shall end. My husband shall be my hero, my lover, my perfect knight. He shall shield me from all care and trouble. He shall ask nothing in return but love—boundless, priceless, rapturous, soul-enthralling love, LOVE! LOVE!! LOVE!!! [*she raves and flings her arms about Fitz*]. And the duties I formerly discharged shall be replaced by the one supreme duty of duties: the duty of weeping at Adolphus's tomb.

FITZ [*reflectively*] My ownest, this sacrifice makes me feel that I have perhaps been a little selfish. I cannot help feeling that there is much to be said for the old arrangement. Why should Adolphus die for my sake?

ADOLPHUS. I am not dying for your sake, Fitz. I am dying because you poisoned me.

MAGNESIA. You do not fear to die, Adolphus, do you?

ADOLPHUS. N-n-no, I dont exactly fear to die. Still—

FITZ. Still, if an antidote—

ADOLPHUS [*bounding from the bed*] Antidote!

MAGNESIA [*with wild hope*] Antidote!

FITZ. If an antidote would not be too much of an anti-climax.

ADOLPHUS. Anti-climax be blowed! Do you think I am going to die to please the critics? Out with your antidote. Quick!

FITZ. The best antidote to the poison I have given you is lime, plenty of lime.

ADOLPHUS. Lime! You mock me! Do you think I carry lime about in my pockets?

FITZ. There is the plaster ceiling.

MAGNESIA. Yes, the ceiling. Saved, saved, saved!

All three frantically shy boots at the ceiling. Flakes of plaster rain down which Adolphus devours, at first ravenously, then with a marked falling off in relish.

MAGNESIA [*picking up a huge slice*] Take this, Adolphus: it is the largest [*she crams it into his mouth*].

FITZ. Ha! a lump off the cornice! Try this.

ADOLPHUS [*desperately*] Stop! stop!

MAGNESIA. Do not stop. You will die. [*She tries to stuff him again*].

ADOLPHUS [*resolutely*] I prefer death.

MAGNESIA and FITZ [*throwing themselves on their knees on either side of him*] For our sakes, Adolphus, persevere.

ADOLPHUS. No: unless you can supply lime in liquid form, I must perish. Finish that ceiling I cannot and will not.

MAGNESIA. I have a thought—an inspiration. My bust. [*She snatches it from its pedestal and brings it to him*].

ADOLPHUS [*gazing fondly at it*] Can I resist it?

FITZ. Try the bun.

ADOLPHUS [*gnawing the knot of hair at the back of the bust's head: it makes him ill*]. Yah, I cannot. I çannot. Not even your bust, Magnesia. Do not ask me. Let me die.

FITZ [*pressing the bust on him*] Force yourself to take a mouthful. Down with it, Adolphus!

ADOLPHUS. Useless. It would not stay down. Water! Some fluid! Ring for something to drink [*he chokes*].

MAGNESIA. I will save you [*she rushes to the bell and rings*].

Phyllis, in her night-gown, with her hair prettily made up into a chevaux de frise of crocuses with pink and yellow curl papers, rushes in straight to Magnesia.

PHYLLIS [*hysterically*] My beloved mistress, once more we

meet. [*She sees Fitztollemache and screams*] Ah! ah! ah! A man!
[*She sees Adolphus*] Men!! [*She flies; but Fitztollemache seizes her
by the night-gown just as she is escaping*]. Unhand me, villain!

FITZ. This is no time for prudery, girl. Mr Bastable is dying.

PHYLLIS [*with concern*] Indeed, sir? I hope he will not think it
unfeeling of me to appear at his deathbed in curl papers.

MAGNESIA. We know you have a good heart, Phyllis. Take this
[*giving her the bust*]; dissolve it in a jug of hot water; and bring it
back instantly. Mr Bastable's life depends on your haste.

PHYLLIS [*hesitating*] It do seem a pity, dont it, my lady, to spoil
your lovely bust?

ADOLPHUS. Tush! This craze for fine art is beyond all bounds.
Off with you [*he pushes her out*]. Drink, drink, drink! My entrails
are parched. Drink! [*he rushes deliriously to the gazogene*].

FITZ [*rushing after him*] Madman, you forget! It is poisoned!

ADOLPHUS. I dont care. Drink, drink! [*They wrestle madly for
the gazogene. In the struggle they squirt all its contents away, mostly
into one another's face. Adolphus at last flings Fitztollemache to the
floor, and puts the spout into his mouth*]. Empty! empty! [*with a
shriek of despair he collapses on the bed, clasping the gazogene like a
baby, and weeping over it*].

FITZ [*aside to Magnesia*] Magnesia: I have always pretended
not to notice it; but you keep a siphon for your private use in my
hat-box.

MAGNESIA. I use it for washing old lace; but no matter: he shall
have it [*she produces a siphon from the hat-box, and offers a tumbler
of soda-water to Adolphus*].

ADOLPHUS. Thanks, thanks, oh, thanks! [*he drinks. A terrific
fizzing is heard. He starts up screaming*] Help! help! The ceiling
is effervescing! I am BURSTING! [*He wallows convulsively on the
bed*].

FITZ. Quick! the rug strap! [*They pack him with blankets and
strap him*]. Is that tight enough?

MAGNESIA [*anxiously*] Will you hold, do you think?

ADOLPHUS. The peril is past. The soda-water has gone flat.

MAGNESIA and FITZ. Thank heaven!

Phyllis returns with a washstand ewer, in which she has dissolved the bust.

MAGNESIA [*snatching it*] At last!

FITZ. You are saved. Drain it to the dregs.

Fitztollemache holds the lip of the ewer to Adolphus's mouth and gradually raises it until it stands upside down. Adolphus's efforts to swallow it are fearful, Phyllis thumping his back when he chokes, and Magnesia loosening the straps when he moans. At last, with a sigh of relief, he sinks back in the women's arms. Fitz shakes the empty ewer upside down like a potman shaking the froth out of a flagon.

ADOLPHUS. How inexpressibly soothing to the chest! A delicious numbness steals through all my members. I would sleep.

MAGNESIA ⎫
FITZ   ⎬ [*whispering*] Let him sleep.
PHYLLIS ⎭

He sleeps. Celestial harps are heard; but their chords cease on the abrupt entrance of the landlord, a vulgar person in pyjamas.

THE LANDLORD. Eah! Eah! Wots this? Wots all this noise? Ah kin ennybody sleep through it? [*Looking at the floor and ceiling*] Ellow! wot you bin doin te maw ceilin?

FITZ. Silence, or leave the room. If you wake that man he dies.

THE LANDLORD. If e kin sleep through the noise you three mikes e kin sleep through ennythink.

MAGNESIA. Detestable vulgarian: your pronunciation jars on the finest chords of my nature. Begone!

THE LANDLORD [*looking at Adolphus*] Aw downt blieve eze esleep. Aw blieve eze dead. [*Calling*] Pleece! Pleece! Merder! [*A blue halo plays mysteriously on the door, which opens and reveals a policeman. Thunder*]. Eah, pleecmin: these three's bin an merdered this gent between em, an naw tore moy ahse dahn.

THE POLICEMAN [*offended*] Policeman, indeed! Wheres your manners?

FITZ. Officer—

THE POLICEMAN [*with distinguished consideration*] Sir?

FITZ. As between gentlemen—

THE POLICEMAN [*bowing*] Sir: to you.

FITZ [*bowing*] I may inform you that my friend had an acute attack of indigestion. No carbonate of soda being available, he swallowed a portion of this man's ceiling. [*Pointing to Adolphus*] Behold the result!

THE POLICEMAN. The ceiling was poisoned! Well, of all the artful— [*he collars the landlord*]. I arrest you for wilful murder.

THE LANDLORD [*appealing to the heavens*] Ow, is this jestice! Ah could aw tell e wiz gowin te eat moy ceilin?

THE POLICEMAN [*releasing him*] True. The case is more complicated than I thought. [*He tries to lift Adolphus's arm but cannot*]. Stiff already.

THE LANDLORD [*trying to lift Adolphus's leg*] An' precious evvy. [*Feeling the calf*] Woy, eze gorn ez awd ez niles.

FITZ [*rushing to the bed*] What is this?

MAGNESIA. Oh, say not he is dead. Phyllis: fetch a doctor. [*Phyllis runs out. They all try to lift Adolphus; but he is perfectly stiff, and as heavy as lead*]. Rouse him. Shake him.

THE POLICEMAN [*exhausted*] Whew! Is he a man or a statue? [*Magnesia utters a piercing scream*]. Whats wrong, Miss?

MAGNESIA [*to Fitz*] Do you not see what has happened?

FITZ [*striking his forehead*] Horror on horror's head!

THE LANDLORD. Wotjemean?

MAGNESIA. The plaster has set inside him. The officer was right: he is indeed a living statue.

Magnesia flings herself on the stony breast of Adolphus. Fitz-tollemache buries his head in his hands; and his chest heaves convulsively. The policeman takes a small volume from his pocket and consults it.

THE POLICEMAN. This case is not provided for in my book of instructions. It dont seem no use trying artificial respiration, do it? [*To the landlord*] Here! lend a hand, you. We'd best take him and set him up in Trafalgar Square.

THE LANDLORD. Aushd pat im in the cestern an worsh it aht of im.

Phyllis comes back with a Doctor.

PHYLLIS. The medical man, my lady.

THE POLICEMAN. A poison case, sir.

THE DOCTOR. Do you mean to say that an unqualified person! a layman! has dared to administer poison in my district?

THE POLICEMAN [*raising Magnesia tenderly*] It looks like it. Hold up, my lady.

THE DOCTOR. Not a moment must be lost. The patient must be kept awake at all costs. Constant and violent motion is necessary.

He snatches Magnesia from the policeman, and rushes her about the room.

FITZ. Stop! That is not the poisoned person!

THE DOCTOR. It is you, then. Why did you not say so before?

He seizes Fitztollemache and rushes him about.

THE LANDLORD. Naow, naow, thet ynt im.

THE DOCTOR. What, you!

He pounces on the landlord and rushes him round.

THE LANDLORD. Eah! chack it. [*He trips the doctor up. Both fall*]. Jest owld this leoonatic, will you, Mister Horficer?

THE POLICEMAN [*dragging both of them to their feet*] Come out of it, will you. You must all come with me to the station.

Thunder.

MAGNESIA. What! In this frightful storm!

The hail patters noisily on the window.

PHYLLIS. I think it's raining.

The wind howls.

THE LANDLORD. It's thanderin and lawtnin.

FITZ. It's dangerous.

THE POLICEMAN [*drawing his baton and whistle*] If you wont come quietly, then—

He whistles. A fearful flash is followed by an appalling explosion of heaven's artillery. A thunderbolt enters the room, and strikes the helmet of the devoted constable, whence it is attracted to the waistcoat of the doctor by the lancet in his pocket. Finally it leaps with fearful force on the landlord, who, being of a gross and spongy nature, absorbs the electric fluid at the cost of his life. The others look on horror-stricken as the three victims, after reeling, jostling, cannoning

202

through a ghastly quadrille, at last sink inanimate on the carpet.

MAGNESIA [*listening at the doctor's chest*] Dead!

FITZ [*kneeling by the landlord, and raising his hand, which drops with a thud*] Dead!

PHYLLIS [*seizing the looking-glass and holding it to the Policeman's lips*] Dead!

FITZ [*solemnly rising*] The copper attracted the lightning.

MAGNESIA [*rising*] After life's fitful fever they sleep well. Phyllis: sweep them up.

Phyllis replaces the looking-glass on the dressing-table; takes up the fan; and fans the policeman, who rolls away like a leaf before the wind to the wall. She disposes similarly of the landlord and doctor.

PHYLLIS. Will they be in your way if I leave them there until morning, my lady? Or shall I bring up the ashpan and take them away?

MAGNESIA. They will not disturb us. Goodnight, Phyllis.

PHYLLIS. Goodnight, my lady. Goodnight, sir.

She retires.

MAGNESIA. And now, husband, let us perform our last sad duty to our friend. He has become his own monument. Let us erect him. He is heavy; but love can do much.

FITZ. A little leverage will get him on his feet. Give me my umbrella.

MAGNESIA. True.

She hands him the umbrella, and takes up the bootjack. They get them under Adolphus's back, and prize him up on his feet.

FITZ. Thats done it! Whew!

MAGNESIA [*kneeling at the left hand of the statue*] For ever and for ever, Adolphus.

FITZ [*kneeling at the right hand of the statue*] The rest is silence.

The Angels sing Bill Bailey. The statue raises its hands in an attitude of blessing, and turns its limelit face to heaven as the curtain falls. National Anthem.

ATTENDANTS [*in front*] All out for the next performance. Pass along, please, ladies and gentlemen: pass along.

THE FASCINATING FOUNDLING

A DISGRACE TO THE AUTHOR

THE FASCINATING FOUNDLING

Morning. Office of the Lord Chancellor. Door on the right leading to his private room, near the fireplace. Door on the left leading to the public staircase. Mercer, an elderly clerk, seated at work. Enter, to him, through the public door, Horace Brabazon, a smart and beautiful young man of nineteen, dressed in the extremity of fashion, with a walking stick.

BRABAZON. I want to see the Lord Chancellor.

MERCER. Have you an appointment?

BRABAZON. No.

MERCER. Then you cant see the Lord Chancellor.

BRABAZON. I tell you I must see him.

MERCER. I tell you you cant. Look here: do you think the Lord Chancellor's a palmist or a hair doctor that people can rush in out of the street and see him whenever they want to?

BRABAZON. That speech was meant to insult and humiliate me. I make it a rule to fight people who attempt to insult and humiliate me. [*Throwing away his stick*] Put up your hands. [*He puts up his own*].

MERCER. Here: you let me alone. You leave this office, d'ye hear; or I'll have the police in on you.

BRABAZON. You are face to face with your destiny; and your destiny is to fight me. Be quick: I'm going to begin. Dont look pale: I scorn to take you by surprise. I shall lead off with my left on your right eye. Put them up.

MERCER. I aint going to fight you. Let me alone, will you? I said nothing to you.

BRABAZON. Liar and slave. Fight, I tell you: fight.

MERCER. Oh, was there ever the like of this? Dont make such a noise.

BRABAZON. I'm making it on purpose. I want you to fight because itll make more noise than anything else. The Lord Chancellor will come to see what the noise is about if only it's loud enough. Time! [*he spars*].

MERCER [*retreating to the fireplace and snatching up the poker*] Ah, would you? You come near me, and I'll split your head open, I will.

BRABAZON [*snatching up the tongs, and engaging him in a stage fight of the noisiest*] Lay on, Macduff; and damned be he that first cries Hold! Enough!

The Lord Chancellor enters indignantly.

THE LORD CHANCELLOR. Whats this? Who is this gentleman?

BRABAZON. The Lord Chancellor. Good. [*To Mercer*] Hence, horrible shadow: unreal mockery, hence. My lord, I have called on professional business. In the matter of Brabazon, an infant.

THE LORD CHANCELLOR. If you are a solicitor, sir, you must be aware that this is not the proper way to approach the Court.

BRABAZON. I approach you as the father of all the orphans in Chancery.

THE LORD CHANCELLOR. Sir—

BRABAZON. Dont fly out: I'll explain everything. You remember the matter of Brabazon, an infant. Come, now! frankly as man to man you do remember the matter of Brabazon, an infant.

THE LORD CHANCELLOR. There is such a case, I believe.

BRABAZON. Of course there is. Well, I'm the infant. I'm Brabazon. I'll call thee Hamlet! King! father! Royal Dane: wilt thou not answer me? [*Prosaically*] Now you see, dont you?

THE LORD CHANCELLOR. You are young Horace Brabazon, are you?

BRABAZON. I am, my lord. Such is life!

THE LORD CHANCELLOR. You are a ward of the Court; and you have systematically disobeyed every order made in your case.

BRABAZON. The orders were unreasonable. Fatuous, in fact.

THE LORD CHANCELLOR. Sir—

BRABAZON. Let me explain. One of the orders was that I was to go into the Church.

THE LORD CHANCELLOR. At your own desire.

BRABAZON. Exactly. But I should not have been indulged. I was too young. How did I know what was good for me? I put it to you as one man to another: do I look like an archbishop?

THE LORD CHANCELLOR. Stuff, sir.

BRABAZON. As you say, nothing could have been more idiotic. You ought to have known better. No: the Church is not in my line. Nature intended me for the stage. The Unreal Mockery here was practising Macduff with me when you came in. Now what I want to know is, can you get me an engagement? As your ward, I have a right to expect that of you. You must know lots of people who could give me a start. And theres another thing: very important. I—Oh, by the way, wont you sit down? Excuse me keeping you standing all this time. Macduff: a chair.

THE LORD CHANCELLOR [with ironic politeness] You are too good. [He sits down].

BRABAZON. Dont mention it. Well, you know: I want some good home influence to steady me. You see you cant steady me: youre too much occupied here with your shop: besides, you may shake a loose leg yourself occasionally for all the public knows, eh? Even if you are virtuous, I should probably lead you astray. No: what I want is a wife. Not a young woman, you know. Someone old enough to be my mother: say thirty or so. I adore a mature woman. Not old enough to be your mother, you understand: old enough to be my mother. I attach some importance to that distinction; so be good enough to bear it in mind. One mustnt overdo these notions.

THE LORD CHANCELLOR. Mr Mercer, will you be good enough to make a careful note of this gentleman's requirements: an engagement at a leading theatre to play Macbeth, and a wife of quiet habits and grave disposition. Anything else, Mr Brabazon?

BRABAZON. Nothing today, thank you. And now, I know better than to take up the time of a busy man. Happy to have made your acquaintance. So long! Ta, ta, Macduff.

He goes out.

THE LORD CHANCELLOR. What do you mean by letting this lunatic in, Mr Mercer? I'm extremely annoyed.

MERCER. I didnt let him in, my lord. He came in. I was keeping him from you at the risk of my life when you came in to ask what the noise was.

THE LORD CHANCELLOR [*with emotion*] My faithful Mercer.

MERCER. My honored master. [*They shake hands, weeping*].

THE LORD CHANCELLOR. We were happy together until this man came between us.

MERCER. Let us try to forget him, my lord. [*Turns to his desk and sees Brabazon's walking stick on the floor*] My lord, he has left his walking stick behind. He will return for it. Let us fly. [*He picks it up and puts it on the desk*].

THE LORD CHANCELLOR. Nonsense, Mercer: we have no aeroplane; and if we had we shouldnt know how to use it. Hark! A visitor at the door. [*They both rush to it. The handle is turned*]. Tell him we have both gone out.

MERCER. Useless, my lord: he is a man of strong reasoning powers: he would conclude, on hearing our voices, that we were both within.

A WOMAN'S VOICE. Is anybody there? Let me in. [*She rattles the door*].

THE LORD CHANCELLOR. That is the voice of a young and probably beautiful woman.

MERCER. It is, my lord.

THE LORD CHANCELLOR. Then why the dickens dont you open the door instead of striking melodramatic attitudes? How dare you keep the lady waiting? I'm very much annoyed.

MERCER. I'm sorry, my lord. [*He opens the door*].

Anastasia Vulliamy enters.

ANASTASIA [*to Mercer*] Is this the Lord Chancellor's?

MERCER. Yes.

ANASTASIA. Sir Cardonius Boshington's?

MERCER. Yes, maam.

ANASTASIA. Are you the Lord Chancellor?

MERCER. No, maam. Leastways, not yet.

ANASTASIA. What are you?

MERCER. I'm the Lord Chancellor's—

ANASTASIA. Secretary?

MERCER. Well, hardly that, maam. If you ask me, I should say I was a sort of what you might call a clerk-valet to his lordship.

ANASTASIA. Are you a gentleman?

MERCER [*staggered*] Well, thats a poser, Miss, really. I'm in a manner of speaking a gentleman.

ANASTASIA. In what manner of speaking are you a gentleman?

MERCER. Well, Miss, I'm a gentleman to my tobacconist. Every man is a gentleman to his tobacconist. The parliamentary candidate for Hornsey always addresses me as a gentleman. But then he aint particular: leastways, not at election times. You see, Miss, there are three classes of gentry in this country.

ANASTASIA. Only three?

MERCER. Only three, maam.

ANASTASIA. How do you tell one from the other?

MERCER. You tell by the railway porters, Miss. The real upper class gives them a shilling; the upper middle class sixpence; and the lower middle, tuppence. I give tuppence myself.

ANASTASIA. And which particular class of gentleman is it, pray, that gives a lady a chair?

MERCER. Oh, I'm sure I beg your pardon, Miss. [*He places a chair for her*].

ANASTASIA. Thanks. And now will you be good enough to tell Sir Cardonius Boshington that Miss Anastasia Vulliamy wishes to see him?

MERCER [*to the Lord Chancellor*] Miss Anaesthesia Vulliamy, my lord, to see you.

ANASTASIA [*springing up*] Do you mean to tell me that this old man in livery is the great Chancellor?

THE LORD CHANCELLOR. At your service, Miss Vulliamy.

ANASTASIA [*producing a newspaper*] Quite impossible. I have here an article on Sir Cardonius, headed Our Great Chancellor; and the description does not correspond in the least. [*Reading*] "No man of our time has succeeded in tempering the awe inspired by a commanding stature and majestic presence with a love and confidence which even the youngest and most timid ward of the Court feels at the sound of his kindly voice and the encouraging beam, twinkling with humor, of his tender grey eyes." Do you mean to tell me that thats you?

THE LORD CHANCELLOR. It is not for me to say how far the description is an accurate or a happy one, madam; but I believe I am the person intended by the writer.

MERCER [*producing another paper*] Perhaps youd recognize this better, Miss. Sir Cardonius and me is on opposite sides in politics.

ANASTASIA [*taking the paper and reading at the place he indicates*] "How much longer will the nation allow this despicable pantaloon to occupy the woolsack—" Whats the woolsack?

MERCER. What the Lord Chancellor sits on in the House of Lords, Miss.

ANASTASIA [*continuing her reading*] "whose contents only too strongly resemble those of his own head." Thats a nasty one, you know: isnt it? It means that your brains are woolly, doesnt it?

THE LORD CHANCELLOR. Its meaning is entirely beneath my notice. I'm surprised, Mercer, to find you in possession of a scurrilous rag of this character. We may differ in our opinions; but if any paper taken in by me were to speak of you in such unbecoming terms, I should never open it again.

MERCER. Well, my lord; politics is politics; and after all, what is politics if it isnt shewing up the other side? When I pay a penny for a paper Ive a right to get value for my money the same as any other man.

ANASTASIA. But I dont understand [*To the Chancellor*] Are you a despicable pantaloon? The other paper says your name will be cherished by the warm hearts of the English people when Eldon and Sir Thomas More are forgotten. I thought that whatever is in the papers must be true. How do you explain being a great Chancellor and a despicable pantaloon at the same time?

THE LORD CHANCELLOR. I take it that the excellent journal from which you first quoted has put all considerations of party aside, and simply endeavored to place before you a dispassionate estimate of such modest services as I have been able to render to my country. The other paper gives you nothing but the vituperative ravings of an illiterate penny-a-liner blinded by party passion.

MERCER. You should never read more than one paper, Miss. It

unsettles the mind, let alone the waste of a penny.

ANASTASIA. Well, it's a great relief to me to hear that the Great Chancellor paper is the right one. [*To the Lord Chancellor*] You think I may believe everything it says?

THE LORD CHANCELLOR. I trust I shall not disappoint any favorable opinion you may have founded on it.

ANASTASIA. It says here that though you are stern with the worthless and merciless to the impostor, yet your mature wisdom and unparalleled legal knowledge are freely at the service of all deserving persons, and that no distressed suitor has ever been turned empty away from your door.

THE LORD CHANCELLOR. That refers to my private house, madam. I dont keep food here.

MERCER. I have a sandwich for my lunch, Miss. Sooner than send you empty away, I would give it to you, Miss, most joyfully.

ANASTASIA. I ask, not charity, but justice.

THE LORD CHANCELLOR. Madam: I must request you to speak like a lady and not like a procession of the unemployed. The House of Lords always gives charity and never gives justice.

MERCER. The House of Lords will find itself unemployed one of these days, if you ask me.

THE LORD CHANCELLOR. Silence, Mercer. Have the goodness to keep your Radicalism to yourself in the presence of this lady.

ANASTASIA. Why do you allow your clerk to be a Radical?

THE LORD CHANCELLOR. Well, madam, to make him a Conservative and an Imperialist I should have to raise his salary very considerably; and I prefer to save money and put up with a Radical.

ANASTASIA. Youll excuse me asking you all these questions; but as Ive decided, after what the paper says, that you are the man to advise me and be a father to me, it's very important that you should be quite all right, isnt it?

THE LORD CHANCELLOR. But it's not my business to be a father to every young lady who walks into my office.

ANASTASIA. Not your business! Why, Whitaker's Almanack

says you get £10,000 a year. You dont get that for nothing, I suppose. [*To Mercer*] By the way, Whitaker doesnt say how much you get.

MERCER. I get one-fifty.

ANASTASIA. One-fifty into £10,000 goes about 66 times. Why does he get 66 times as much as you? Is he sixty-six times as good?

MERCER. He thinks so.

THE LORD CHANCELLOR. I set up no such ridiculous pretension, Mercer.

ANASTASIA [*to the Lord Chancellor*] Perhaps youre 66 times as sober. How much do you drink every day?

THE LORD CHANCELLOR. I am almost a teetotaller. A single bottle of burgundy is quite sufficient for me.

ANASTASIA [*to Mercer*] Then I suppose you drink 66 bottles of burgundy a day.

MERCER. 66 bottles of burgundy a day on one-fifty a year! Not me. It hardly runs to beer on Sundays.

ANASTASIA. Well, there must be something awfully wrong about you, you know, if you get only the sixty-sixth of what he gets.

THE LORD CHANCELLOR. No, madam. Mercer is an excellent man in his proper place.

ANASTASIA. Then there must be something awfully right about you.

THE LORD CHANCELLOR. I hope so.

ANASTASIA. I dont see the difference myself.

MERCER. He's better fed.

ANASTASIA. Is he? I should have thought he was too red about the nose to be quite healthy. It's the burgundy, I expect. However, I didnt come here to talk about you two. Call it selfish if you will; but I came to talk about myself. The fact is, I'm an orphan. At least, I think I am.

THE LORD CHANCELLOR. Dont you know?

ANASTASIA. No. I was brought up in what you might politely call a sort of public institution. They found me on the doorstep, you know. Might have happened to anybody, mightnt it?

MERCER [*scandalized*] And you have the audacity to come here and talk up to us as if you was a lady. Be off with you; and be ashamed of yourself, you hussy.

THE LORD CHANCELLOR. Gently, Mercer, gently. It is not the poor girl's fault.

MERCER. Not her fault! Why, she aint anybody's daughter: she's only an offspring.

ANASTASIA. Perhaps I'm his daughter, my lord.

MERCER. Oh, you wicked girl! Oh, you naughty story, you! Oh, that I should have lived to have this accusation brought against me: me! a respectable man!

ANASTASIA. I had a feeling the moment I saw you.

THE LORD CHANCELLOR. The voice of Nature! Oh, Mercer, Mercer!

MERCER. I'll have the law of you for this, I will. Oh, say you dont believe her, my lord. Dont drive me mad. Say you dont believe her.

THE LORD CHANCELLOR. I cant disregard the voice of Nature, Mercer. The evidence against you is very black.

MERCER. Me the father of a common girl found on a workhouse doorstep!

ANASTASIA [*rising most indignantly*] How dare you presume to say such a thing? A workhouse doorstep indeed! I was found on the doorstep of one of the very best houses in Park Lane.

THE LORD CHANCELLOR [*overwhelmed*] My dear young lady, how can I apologize—

MERCER [*crushed*] I'm sure I beg your pardon most humbly, Miss.

THE LORD CHANCELLOR. Forget the rudeness of my clerk: he knows no better. Resume your seat, I beg.

MERCER. If I had only known, Miss! Park Lane! I could bite my tongue out for my bad manners, I do assure you.

ANASTASIA. Say no more. Of course you could not know my social position.

MERCER. Dont say that, Miss. You have Park Lane in every

feature.

THE LORD CHANCELLOR [*effusively*] In your manners.

MERCER. In your accent.

THE LORD CHANCELLOR. In your tone—

MERCER. Address—

THE LORD CHANCELLOR. A je ne sais quoi—

MERCER. A tout ensemble—

ANASTASIA. You speak French?

MERCER. Not a word, Miss; but at the sight of that hat of yours the French fairly burst out of me.

ANASTASIA. You are very good—

THE LORD CHANCELLOR } Oh, not at all.

MERCER. } Dont mention it.

ANASTASIA. Dont begin again. I forgive you both. Now, attention! I'm a good-hearted but somewhat flighty girl; and I require some serious interest in life to steady me. As I had an ungovernable appetite, and was naturally rather inclined to be stout, I tried politics. For you, a man, politics meant the House of Lords. For me, a woman, politics meant Holloway Gaol and the hunger strike. I refused to take food until I was so frightfully hungry that when the Governor—who was a plump, chubby, tempting sort of man, you know—came into my cell and remonstrated with me, I attempted to devour him.

THE LORD CHANCELLOR. Pardon me. I thought you Suffragist lambs prided yourselves on acting always on principle. On what principle, may I ask, do you justify an attempt to devour an estimable public official?

ANASTASIA. On the Cat and Mouse principle, my lord. That is a part of the law of England.

MERCER. Never. Not when the woman is the cat.

THE LORD CHANCELLOR. May I ask, madam, what the unfortunate mouse did on this occasion?

ANASTASIA. He got quite angry, and said he wouldnt have me in his prison another minute—not if I went down on my knees and begged him to let me stay. Of course I refused to go; but I had to let the poor man have his way at last, though it took ten wardresses to persuade me to do it. I left them simply in ribbons, poor things. Prison made a great change in me. Before I went in I felt a great want of something to love; but when I came out I felt nothing but a great want of something to eat. There were two public houses near the prison. One had a placard up "Sausage and Mashed," the other "Sandwich and Small Lloyd George." I visited both in succession, and had two goes of each delicacy. I then drove to the Holborn Restaurant and had a five shilling lunch, stopping at three Pearce and Plentys on the way to sustain exhausted nature. At the Holborn they refused to serve me with a second lunch; so I went on to the Carlton. Of my subsequent experiences at the Savoy, Pagani's, Frascati's, Gatti's, five baked potato men, and a coffee stall, I shall say nothing. Suffice it that when at last the craving for food was stilled, the craving for love returned in all its original force. I felt I must have something to cherish, to sacrifice myself for. You no doubt hold that self-sacrifice is a woman's chief amusement.

THE LORD CHANCELLOR. Certainly I do.

ANASTASIA. Any man would. Well, what was I to love? My friends recommended marriage: a man, in fact. But I hesitated to rush at once to so expensive and troublesome an extreme. I tried a pet dog; but when it had been stolen for the sixth time by the man I bought it from, I refused to pay any more rewards, and we were parted for ever. I tried a cat; but its conduct was so disreputable that I really could not live in the same house with it. I adopted the orphan child of a crossing sweeper who was run over; but when its aunt learnt that I had no parents she would not permit it to stay. Glad as I must confess I was to get rid of the little beast, my starved heart still ached, my empty arms still longed to gather some beloved object to my breast.

THE LORD CHANCELLOR. If I can be of any service to you, madam—

ANASTASIA. You? You are married, are you not?

THE LORD CHANCELLOR. Well, er, yes I er—am married.

MERCER [catching her eye] I'm sorry, miss; but so am I. Still, a divorce would be a matter of only eighty pound or so if we made it a fairly straight case.

ANASTASIA. Never shall it be said that Anastasia Vulliamy built her happiness on the ruin of another woman's home. There are younger and handsomer men than you, my lord: there are more genteel characters than Mercer. Neither of you, if I may be allowed the expression, is precisely what I should call a peach. And I want—oh, I want a peach. He must be a young peach. Not that I am to be seduced by the fleeting charms of a smooth cheek and a slim figure. But it's a necessity of my position as a woman that I should marry someone whom I can bully, because if a woman cant bully her husband, her husband generally bullies her.

> You, my lord, you will, you can,
> Find me a young and foolish man.
> Into my arms: under my thumb
> Let him come, let him come.

I fear I am almost dropping into poetry; but the tumult of my emotions carries me away. I implore you not to keep me waiting. My soul, my soul is thrilling as it never thrilled before. My arms, my arms are longing as they never longed before. My heart, my heart is beating as it never bet before. Every nerve in my body, every fibre in my heart—

Brabazon enters.

BRABAZON. Excuse me: I left my stick, I think—

ANASTASIA [*throwing herself into his arms*] He has come: he has come: the very thing I want.

BRABAZON. Quite out of the question, my dear lady. Sir Cardonius will tell you that you are too young, too irresponsible, too impulsive to be anything more to me than an extremely agreeable object of contemplation, and a charming hostess. With that object may I venture to propose a marriage to you?

ANASTASIA. Silly! that is exactly what *I* am proposing to you.

BRABAZON. Not marriage to the same person, I think. You, as I understand it, propose to marry me. *I* propose that you should marry one of my friends. You can then invite me to your house, and put on your best company manners for my benefit. He will have the privilege of paying for your hats, and enjoying your no-company manners.

MERCER. My lord: this man has a giant intellect.

THE LORD CHANCELLOR. It will avail him as little as if he were the biggest fool in creation. Young man: you are lost. I argued as you do. I tried to get out of it.

MERCER. I moved all the way from Gospel Oak to Islington to escape; but it was no use.

THE LORD CHANCELLOR. Beware how you anger her by shewing any reluctance. Remember: "Hell hath no fury like a woman scorned."

MERCER. Whats the good of that nowadays? When that was written a woman would take no for an answer. She wont now.

ANASTASIA. You will begin walking out with me at once. You are only on approval, of course; but if you suit, you may consider next Friday three weeks named as the day.

BRABAZON. But where does the merit come in for me? Where is the moral discipline? Where is the self-sacrifice? You are an agreeable person: to marry you would be an act of pure selfishness.

ANASTASIA. So you think now, dearest. You wont think that a year hence. I'll take care of that for my own boy.

BRABAZON. Yes, but look here, you know. Have you any money?

ANASTASIA. Not a rap.

BRABAZON. And you expect to get a slave for nothing. What cheek!

ANASTASIA. I'm richer than you think, darling. It's true that I'm a poor penniless orphan. Doesnt that touch you?

BRABAZON. Not in the least.

ANASTASIA. Thoughtless boy. Have you forgotten that the women who have money always belong to some family or other?

BRABAZON. Well?

ANASTASIA. Well, a family means relations. You cant call your house your own. The brothers borrow money. The sisters come and stay for months. The mother quarrels with your mother.

MERCER. Gospel truth, every word of it.

THE LORD CHANCELLOR. Undeniable. [*He sighs deeply*].

ANASTASIA. I, my love, am not perfect. I am a weak woman: I have nothing to cling to but your love, nor any place to rest except your very becoming fancy waistcoat. But at least I'm a foundling.

BRABAZON [*excited and hopeful*] A foundling?

ANASTASIA. I havnt a relation in the world.

BRABAZON [*clasping her*] Mine! mine! MINE!!!

AYOT ST LAWRENCE, 10*th August* 1909.

THE MUSIC-CURE
A PIECE OF UTTER NONSENSE

THIS is not a serious play: it is what is called a Variety Turn for two musicians. It is written for two pianists, but can be adapted to any instruments on which the performers happen to be proficient. At its first performance by Miss Madge McIntosh and Mr William Armstrong the difficulty arose that, though Mr Armstrong was an accomplished pianist, Miss McIntosh's virtuosity was confined to the English concertina. That did just as well.

As a last desperate resort a pianola behind the scenes can be employed; but the result will lack spontaneity.

There is, however, no pressing reason why the thing should be performed at all.

THE MUSIC-CURE

Lord Reginald Fitzambey, a fashionably dressed, rather pretty young man of 22, is prostrate on a sofa in a large hotel drawing room, crying convulsively. His doctor is trying to soothe him. The doctor is about a dozen years his senior; and his ways are the ways of a still youthful man who considers himself in smart society as well as professionally attendant on it.

The drawing room has tall central doors, at present locked. If anyone could enter under these circumstances, he would find on his left a grand piano with the keyboard end towards him, and a smaller door beyond the piano. On his right would be the window, and, further on, the sofa on which the unhappy youth is wallowing, with, close by it, the doctor's chair and a little table accommodating the doctor's hat, a plate, a medicine bottle, a half emptied glass, and a bell call.

THE DOCTOR. Come come! be a man. Now really this is silly. You mustnt give way like this. I tell you nothing's happened to you. Hang it all! it's not the end of the world if you did buy a few shares—

REGINALD [*interrupting him frantically*] I never meant any harm in buying those shares. I am ready to give them up. Oh, I never meant any harm in buying those shares. I never meant any harm in buying those shares. [*Clutching the doctor imploringly*] Wont you believe me, Doctor? I never meant any harm in buying those shares. I never—

THE DOCTOR [*extricating himself and replacing Reginald on the couch, not very gently*] Of course you didnt. I know you didnt.

REGINALD. I never—

THE DOCTOR [*desperate*] Dont go on saying that over and over again or you will drive us all as distracted as you are yourself. This is nothing but nerves. Remember that youre in a hotel. Theyll put you out if you make a row.

REGINALD [*tearfully*] But you dont understand. Oh, why wont anybody understand? I never—

THE DOCTOR [*shouting him down*] You never meant any harm

in buying those shares. This is the four hundreth time youve said it.

REGINALD [*wildly*] Then why do you keep asking me the same questions over and over again? It's not fair. Ive told you I never meant any harm in——

THE DOCTOR. Yes, yes, yes: I know, I know. You think you made a fool of yourself before that committee. Well, you didnt. You stood up to it for six days with the coolness of an iceberg and the cheerfulness of an idiot. Every member of it had a go at you; and everyone of them, including some of the cleverest cross-examiners in London, fell back baffled before your fatuous self-satisfaction, your impenetrable inability to see any reason why you shouldnt have bought those shares.

REGINALD. But why shouldnt I have bought them? I made no secret of it. When the Prime Minister ragged me about it I offered to sell him the shares for what I gave for them.

THE DOCTOR. Yes, after they had fallen six points. But never mind that. The point for you is that you are an under-secretary in the War Office. You knew that the Army was going to be put on vegetarian diet, and that the British Maccaroni Trust shares would go up with a rush when this became public. And what did you do?

REGINALD. I did what any fellow would have done. I bought all the shares I could afford.

THE DOCTOR. You bought a great many more than you could afford.

REGINALD. But why shouldnt I? Explain it to me. I'm anxious to learn. I meant no harm. I see no harm. Why am I to be badgered because the beastly Opposition papers and all the Opposition rotters on that committee try to make party capital out of it by saying that it was disgraceful? It wasnt disgraceful: it was simple common sense. I'm not a financier; but you cant persuade me that if you happen to know that certain shares are going to rise you shouldnt buy them. It would be flying in the face of Providence not to. And they wouldnt see that. They pretended not to see it. They worried me, and kept asking me the same thing over and over again, and wrote blackguardly articles about me——

THE DOCTOR. And you got the better of them all because you couldnt see their point of view. But what beats me is why you broke down afterwards.

REGINALD. Everyone was against me. I thought the committee a pack of fools; and I as good as told them so. But everyone took their part. The governor said I had disgraced the family name. My brothers said I ought to resign from my clubs. My mother said that all her hopes of marrying me to a rich woman were shattered. And I'd done nothing: absolutely nothing to what other chaps are doing every day.

THE DOCTOR. Well, the long and short of it is that officials mustnt gamble.

REGINALD. But I wasnt gambling. I knew. It isnt gambling if you know that the shares will go up. It's a cert.

THE DOCTOR. Well, all I can tell you is that if you werent a son of the Duke of Dunmow, youd have to resign; and—

REGINALD [breaking down] Oh, stop talking to me about it. Let me alone. I cant bear it. I never meant any harm in buying those shares. I never meant any harm—

THE DOCTOR. Sh-sh-sh-sh-sh! There: I shouldnt have started the subject again. Take some of this valerian [he puts the glass to Reginald's lips]. Thats right. Now youre better.

REGINALD [exhausted but calm] Why does valerian soothe me when it excites cats? Theres a question to reflect on! You know, they ought to have made me a philosopher.

THE DOCTOR. Philosophers are born, not made.

REGINALD. Fine old chestnut, that. Everybody's born, not made.

THE DOCTOR. Youre getting almost clever. I dont like it: youre not yourself today. I wish I could take your mind off your troubles. Suppose you try a little music.

REGINALD. I cant play. My fingers wont obey me. And I cant stand the sound of the piano. I sounded a note this morning; and it made me scream.

THE DOCTOR. But why not get somebody to play to you?

REGINALD. Whom could I get, even if I could bear it? You

cant play.

THE DOCTOR. Well: I'm not the only person in the world.

REGINALD. If you bring anyone else in here, I shall go mad. I'll throw myself out of the window. I cant bear the idea of music. I dread it, hate it, loathe it.

THE DOCTOR. Thats very serious, you know.

REGINALD. Why is it serious?

THE DOCTOR. Well, what would become of you without your turn for music? You have absolutely no capacity in any other direction.

REGINALD. I'm in Parliament. And I'm an under-secretary.

THE DOCTOR. Thats because your father is a Duke. If you were in a Republic you wouldnt be trusted to clean boots, unless your father was a millionaire. No, Reginald: the day you give up vamping accompaniments and playing the latest ragtimes by ear, youre a lost man socially.

REGINALD [*deprecating*] Oh, I say!

THE DOCTOR [*rising*] However, perhaps it's too soon for you to try the music-cure yet. It was your mother's idea; but I'll call and tell her to wait a day or two. I think she meant to send somebody to play. I must be off now. Look in again later. Meanwhile, sleep as much as you can. Or you might read a little.

REGINALD. What can I read?

THE DOCTOR. Try the Strand Magazine.

REGINALD. But it's so frightfully intellectual. It would overtax my brain.

THE DOCTOR. Oh, well, I suppose it would. Well, sleep. Perhaps I'd better give you something to send you off [*he produces a medicine case*].

REGINALD. Whats this? Veronal?

THE DOCTOR. Dont be alarmed. Only the old-fashioned remedy: opium. Take this [*Reginald takes a pill*]: that will do the trick, I expect. If you find after half an hour that it has only excited you, take another. I'll leave one for you [*he puts one on the plate, and pockets his medicine case*].

REGINALD. Better leave me a lot. I like pills.

THE DOCTOR. Thank you: I'm not treating you with a view to a coroner's inquest. You know, dont you, that opium is a poison?

REGINALD. Yes, opium. But not pills.

THE DOCTOR. Well, Heaven forbid that I, a doctor, should shake anybody's faith in pills. But I shant leave you enough to kill you. [*He puts on his hat*].

REGINALD. Youll tell them, wont you, not to let anyone in. Really and truly I shall throw myself out of the window if any stranger comes in. I should go out of my mind.

THE DOCTOR. None of us have very far to go to do that, my young friend. Ta ta, for the moment [*he makes for the central doors*].

REGINALD. You cant go out that way. I made my mother lock it and take away the key. I felt sure theyd let somebody in that way if she didnt. Youll have to go the way you came.

THE DOCTOR [*returning*] Right. Now let me see you settle down before I go. I want you to be asleep before I leave the room.

Reginald settles himself to sleep with his face to the back of the sofa. The doctor goes softly to the side door and goes out.

REGINALD [*sitting up wildly and staring affrightedly at the piano*] Doctor! Doctor! Help!!!

THE DOCTOR [*returning hastily*] What is it?

REGINALD [*after another doubtful look at the piano*] Nothing. [*He composes himself to sleep again*].

THE DOCTOR. Nothing! There must have been something or you wouldnt have yelled like that. [*Pulling Reginald over so as to see his face*] Here! what was it?

REGINALD. Well, it's gone.

THE DOCTOR. Whats gone?

REGINALD. The crocodile.

THE DOCTOR. The crocodile!

REGINALD. Yes. It laughed at me, and was going to play the piano with its tail.

THE DOCTOR. Opium in small doses doesnt agree with you, my young friend. [*Taking the spare pill from the plate*] I shall have to give you a second pill.

REGINALD. But suppose two crocodiles come!

THE DOCTOR. They wont. If anything comes it will be something pretty this time. Thats how opium acts. Anyhow, youll be fast asleep in ten minutes. Here. Take it.

REGINALD [*after taking the pill*] It was awfully silly of me. But you know I really saw the thing.

THE DOCTOR. You neednt trouble about what you see with your eyes shut. [*He turns to the door*].

REGINALD. Would you mind looking under the sofa to make sure the crocodile isnt there?

THE DOCTOR. Why not look yourself? that would be more convincing.

REGINALD. I darent.

THE DOCTOR. You duffer! [*He looks*]. All serene. No crocodile. Now go bye bye. [*He goes out*].

Reginald again composes himself to sleep. Somebody unlocks the central doors. A lovely lady enters with a bouquet in her hand. She looks about her; takes a letter from wherever she carries letters; and starts on a voyage of discovery round the room, checking her observations by the contents of the letter. The piano seems specially satisfactory: she nods as she sees it. Reginald seems also to be quite expected. She does not speak to him. When she is quite satisfied that she is in the right room, she goes to the piano and tantalizes the expectant audience for about two minutes by putting down her flowers on the candle-stand; taking off her gloves and putting them with the flowers; taking off half a dozen diamond rings in the same way; sitting down to the keyboard and finding it too near to the piano, then too far, then too high, then too low: in short, exhausting all the tricks of the professional pianist before she at last strikes the keys and preludes brilliantly. At the sound, Reginald, with a scream, rolls from the sofa and writhes on the carpet in horrible contortions. She stops playing, amazed.

REGINALD. Oh! Oh! Oh! The crocodiles! Stop! Ow! Oh! [*He looks at the piano and sees the lady*] Oh I say!

THE LADY. What on earth do you mean by making that noise

when I'm playing? Have you no sense? Have you no manners?

REGINALD [*sitting on the floor*] I'm awfully sorry.

THE LADY. Sorry! Why did you do it?

REGINALD. I thought you were a crocodile.

THE LADY. What a silly thing to say! Do I look like a crocodile?

REGINALD. No.

THE LADY. Do I play like a crocodile!

REGINALD [*cautiously rising and approaching her*] Well, You know, it's so hard to know how a crocodile would play.

THE LADY. Stuff! [*She resumes her playing*].

REGINALD. Please! [*He stops her by shutting the keyboard lid*]. Who let you in?

THE LADY [*rising threateningly*] What is that to you, pray?

REGINALD [*retreating timidly*] It's my room, you know.

THE LADY. It's nothing of the sort. It's the Duchess of Dunmow's room. I know it's the right one, because she gave me the key; and it was the right key.

REGINALD. But what did she do that for? Who are you, if you dont mind my asking?

THE LADY. I do mind your asking. It's no business of yours. However, youd better know to whom you are speaking. I am Strega Thundridge. [*She pronounces it Strayga*].

REGINALD. What! The female Paderewski!

STREGA. Pardon me. I believe Mr Paderewski has been called the male Thundridge; but no gentleman would dream of repeating such offensive vulgarities. Will you be good enough to return to your sofa, and hold your tongue, or else leave the room.

REGINALD. But, you know, I am ill.

STREGA. Then go to bed, and send for a doctor. [*She sits down again to the keyboard*].

REGINALD [*falling on his knees*] You mustnt play. You really mustnt. I cant stand it. I shall simply not be myself if you start playing.

STREGA [*raising the lid*] Then I shall start at once.

REGINALD [*running to her on his knees and snatching at her hands*] No, you shant. [*She rises indignantly. He holds on to her hands, but exclaims ecstatically*] Oh, I say, what lovely hands youve got!

STREGA. The idea! [*She hurls him to the carpet*].

REGINALD. [*on the floor staring at her*] You are strong.

STREGA. My strength has been developed by playing left hand octave passages—like this. [*She begins playing Liszt's transcription of Schubert's Erl König*].

REGINALD [*puts his fingers in his ears, but continues to stare at her*].

STREGA [*stopping*] I really cannot play if you keep your ears stopped. It is an insult. Leave the room.

REGINALD. But I tell you it's my room.

STREGA [*rising*] Leave the room, or I will ring your bell and have you put out. [*She goes to the little table, and poises her fingers over the bell call*].

REGINALD [*rushing to her*] No no: somebody will come if you ring; and I shall go distracted if a stranger comes in. [*With a touch of her left hand she sends him reeling. He appeals to her plaintively*] Dont you see that I am ill?

STREGA. I see that you are mentally afflicted. But that doesnt matter to me. The Duchess of Dunmow has engaged me to come to this room and play for two hours. I never break an engagement, especially a two hundred and fifty guinea one. [*She turns towards the piano*].

REGINALD. But didnt she tell you anything about me?

STREGA [*turning back to him*] She said there would be a foolish young man in the room, but that I was not to mind him. She assured me you were not dangerous except to yourself. [*Collaring him and holding him bent backwards over the piano*]. But I will have no nonsense about not listening. All the world listens when I play. Listen, or go.

REGINALD [*helpless*] But I shall have to sit on the stairs. I darent go into any of the rooms: I should meet people there.

STREGA. You will meet plenty of people on the stairs, young man. They are sitting six on each stair, not counting those who

230

are sitting astride the banisters on the chance of hearing me play.

REGINALD. How dreadful! [*Tearfully*] Youve no right to bully me like this. I'm ill: I cant bear it. I'll throw myself out of the window.

STREGA [*releasing him*] Do. What an advertisement! It will be really kind of you. [*She goes back to the keyboard and sits down to play*].

REGINALD [*crossing to the window*] Youll be sorry you were so unfeeling when you see my mangled body. [*He opens the window; looks out; shuts it hastily, and retreats with a scream*]. Theres a crowd. I darent.

STREGA [*pleased*] Waiting to hear me play [*she preludes softly*].

REGINALD [*ravished*] Oh! I can stand that, you know.

STREGA [*ironically, still preluding*] Thank you.

REGINALD. The fact is, I can play a bit myself.

STREGA [*still preluding*] An amateur, I presume.

REGINALD. I have often been told I could make a living at it if I tried. But of course it wouldnt do for a man in my position to lower himself by becoming a professional.

STREGA [*abruptly ceasing to play*] Tactful, that, I dont think! And what do you play, may I ask?

REGINALD. Oh, all the very best music.

STREGA. For instance?

REGINALD. I wish you belonged to me.

STREGA [*rising outraged*] You young blackguard! How dare you?

REGINALD. You dont understand: it's the name of a tune. Let me play it for you. [*He sits down at the keyboard*] I dont think you believe I can play.

STREGA. Pardon me. I have heard a horse play the harmonium at a music hall. I can believe anything.

REGINALD. Aha! [*He plays*]. Do you like that?

STREGA. What is it? Is it intended for music?

REGINALD. Oh, you beautiful doll.

STREGA. Take that [*she knocks him sprawling over the keyboard*]! Beautiful doll indeed!

REGINALD. Oh, I say! Look here: thats the name of the tune too. You seem quite ignorant of the best music. Dont you know Rum Tum Tiddle, and Alexander's Rag Time Band, and Take me back to the Garden of Love, and Everybody likes our Mary.

STREGA. Young man: I have never even heard of these abominations. I am now going to educate you musically. I am going to play Chopin, and Brahms, and Bach, and Schumann, and—

REGINALD [*horrified*] You dont mean classical music?

STREGA. I do [*he bolts through the central doors*].

STREGA [*disgusted*] Pig! [*She sits down at the piano again*].

REGINALD [*rushing back into the room*] I forgot the people on the stairs: crowds of them. Oh, what shall I do! Oh dont, Dont, Dont play classical music to me. Say you wont. Please.

STREGA [*looks at him enigmatically and softly plays a Liebeslieder Waltz*]!!

REGINALD. Oh, I say: thats rather pretty.

STREGA. Like it?

REGINALD. Awfully. Oh, I say, you know: I really do wish you belonged to me. [*Strega suddenly plays a violent Chopin study. He goes into convulsions*]. Oh! Stop! Mercy! Help! Oh please, please!

STREGA [*pausing with her hands raised over the keyboard, ready to pounce on the chords*] Will you ever say that again?

REGINALD. Never. I beg your pardon.

STREGA [*satisfied*] Hm! [*She drops her hands in her lap*].

REGINALD [*wiping his brow*] Oh, that was fearfully classical.

STREGA. You want your back stiffened a little, my young friend. Besides, I really cannot earn two hundred and fifty guineas by playing soothing syrup to you. Now prepare for the worst. I'm going to make a man of you.

REGINALD. How?

STREGA. With Chopin's Polonaise in A Flat. Now. Imagine yourself going into battle. [*He runs away as before*] Goose!

REGINALD [*returning as before*] The crowd is worse than ever. Have you no pity?

STREGA. Come here. Dont imagine yourself going into battle.

Imagine that you have just been in a battle; and that you have saved your country by deeds of splendid bravery; and that you are going to dance with beautiful women who are proud of you. Can you imagine that?

REGINALD. Rathe-e-e-errr. Thats how I always do imagine myself.

STREGA. Right. Now listen. [*She plays the first section of the Polonaise. Reginald flinches at first, but gradually braces himself; stiffens; struts; throws up his head and slaps his chest*]. Thats better. What a hero! [*After a difficult passage*]. Takes a bit of doing, that, dearest child. [*Coming to the chords which announce the middle section*] Now for it.

REGINALD [*unable to contain himself*] Oh, this is too glorious. I must have a turn or I shall forget myself.

STREGA. Can you play this? Nothing but this. [*She plays the octave passage in the bass*].

REGINALD. Just riddle tiddle, riddle tiddle, riddle tiddle, riddle tiddle? Nothing but that?

STREGA. Very softly at first. Like the ticking of a watch. Then louder and louder, as you feel my soul swelling.

REGINALD. I understand. Just give me those chords again to buck me up to it. [*She plays the chords again. He plays the octave passages; and they play the middle section as a duet. At the repeat he cries*] Again! again!

STREGA. It's meant to be played again. Now.

They repeat it. At the end of the section she pushes him off the bench on to the floor, and goes on with the Polonaise alone.

REGINALD. Wonderful woman: I have a confession to make, a confidence to impart. Your playing draws it from me. Listen, Strega [*she plays a horrible discord*] I mean Miss Thundridge.

STREGA. Thats better; but I prefer Wonderful Woman.

REGINALD. You are a wonderful woman, you know. Adored one—would you mind my taking a little valerian? I'm so excited [*he takes some*]. A—a—ah! Now I feel that I can speak. Listen to me, goddess. I am not happy. I hate my present existence. I loathe parliament. I am not fit for public affairs. I am condemned to live at home with five coarse and brutal sisters who care for nothing but Alpine climbing, and looping the loop on aeroplanes, and going on deputations, and fighting the police. Do you know what they call me?

STREGA [*playing softly*] What do they call you, dear?

REGINALD. They call me a Clinger. Well, I confess it. I am a Clinger. I am not fit to be thrown unprotected upon the world. I want to be shielded. I want a strong arm to lean on, a dauntless heart to be gathered to and cherished, a breadwinner on whose income I can live without the sordid horrors of having to make money for myself. I am a poor little thing, I know, Strega; but I could make a home for you. I have great taste in carpets and pictures. I can cook like anything. I can play quite nicely after dinner. Though you mightnt think it, I can be quite stern and strongminded with servants. I get on splendidly with children: they never talk over my head as grown-up people do. I have a real genius for home life. And I shouldnt at all mind being tyrannized over a little: in fact, I like it. It saves me the trouble of having to think what to do. Oh, Strega, dont you want a dear little domesticated husband who would have no concern but to please you, no thought outside our home, who would be unspotted and unsoiled by the rude cold world, who would never meddle in politics or annoy you by interfering with your profession? Is there any hope for me?

STREGA [*coming away from the piano*] My child: I am a hard, strong, independent, muscular woman. How can you, with your delicate soft nature, see anything to love in me? I should hurt you, shock you, perhaps—yes: let me confess it—I have a violent temper, and might even, in a transport of rage, beat you.

REGINALD. Oh do, do. Dont laugh at this ridiculous confession; but ever since I was a child I have had only one secret longing, and that was to be mercilessly beaten by a splendid, strong, beautiful woman.

STREGA [*solemnly*] Reginald—I think your mother spoke of you as Reginald?—

REGINALD. Rejjy.

STREGA. I too have a confession to make. I too need some music to speak through. Will you be so good?

REGINALD. Angel. [*He rushes to the piano and plays sympathetically whilst she speaks*].

STREGA. I, too, have had my dream. It has consoled me through the weary hours when I practised scales for eight hours a day. It has pursued me through the applause of admiring thousands in Europe and America. It is a dream of a timid little heart fluttering against mine, of a gentle voice to welcome me home, of a silky moustache to kiss my weary fingers when I return from a Titanic struggle with Tchaikovsky's Concerto in G major, of somebody utterly dependent on me, utterly devoted to me, utterly my own, living only to be cherished and worshipped by me.

REGINALD. But you would be angry sometimes: terrible, splendid, ruthless, violent. You would throw down the thing you loved and trample on it as it clung to your feet.

STREGA. Yes—oh, why do you force me to confess it?—I should beat it to a jelly, and then cast myself in transports of remorse on its quivering frame and smother it with passionate kisses.

REGINALD [*transported*] Let it be me, let it be me.

STREGA. You dare face this terrible destiny?

REGINALD. I embrace it. I adore you. I am wholly yours. Oh, let me cling, cling, cling.

STREGA [*embracing him fiercely*] Nothing shall tear you from my arms now.

REGINALD. Nothing. I am provided for. Oh how happy this will make my mother!

STREGA. Sweet: name the day.

He plays a wedding march. She plays the bass.

AYOT ST LAWRENCE, 21*st January* 1914.

THE END